Uniquely Called

Live Out Your Faith in the Marketplace

Brian C. Dobbs

CONTENTS

ACKNOWLEDGMENTS

Thank you Shannon for being a wonderful wife, helpmate, prayer warrior and best friend. You have been by my side every step of the way, loving me unconditionally and being the encouragement I needed to press through and accomplish all that's in my heart.

I want to thank James Brooks, who is our good friend and amazing photographer; as well as a special and sincere note of appreciation to my friends, family and clients who have added so much joy to my life.

INTRODUCTION

"I brought glory to you here on earth by completing the work you gave me to do." John 17:4 NLT

Uniquely Called is a thrilling journey—movie worthy with all the challenges, obstacles, and peak-and-valley moments. Emotions are on display and gut-wrenching scenes that make you sit on the edge of your seat. It's filled with victories and setbacks, along with the educational moments where the character regains the grit to press forward. Relentless in pursuit, the mission must be accomplished. Lives will be touched, saved, and ultimately the shift in culture creates a better place for others.

      Uniquely Called is about you and your story. Everyone has a calling, and the ones who are receptive take the plunge into a life that is far different than the status quo. They are who you and I look like when we tap into the assignment that we have from the Lord. Not knowing all that it would take, many have jumped in with both feet to pioneer the uncharted course to fulfill this heart craving.

1

Their lives were an example, inspiration and motivation for others to follow. Will you accept the Call?

Uniquely Called is more than a mission statement. It is the fuel that propels you forward. **Uniquely Called** is the passion inside of you that desires to see things reconciled, restored, redeemed and rebuilt. It takes getting better personally in all areas, not just one. It's a desire to be the person who God created you to be; not wanting to leave anything on the table, so to speak, and completely determined to maximize your potential and experience the abundant life that God has for you.

"Beloved friend, I pray that you are prospering in every way and that you continually enjoy good health, just as your soul is prospering." 3 John 2 TPT

Along with your desire, another vital component is the need for good laid out plans, strategies, finances and connections to accomplish the mission. These will serve as the catalyst for exchange. The business conducted now becomes Kingdom business.

"Let your light so shine before men, that they may see your good works and glorify your Father in heaven." Matthew 5:16 NKJV

Next, your personal walk with God is and must remain the cornerstone of your life. After all, God is the One who placed this calling in your heart originally, and it is imperative to continue to seek Him for guidance in this journey. There is power in knowing the Lord works beside you and manifests Himself in your day to day activities. This combination of personal, professional and spiritual dimensions all working together creates a powerful force to be reckoned with.

"It is through him that we live and function and have our identity; just as your own poets have said, 'Our lineage comes from him." Acts 17:28 TPT

As you read this book, you will journey through two parts. Part One gives you a brief glimpse of the process I went through personally. You will get to know the behind-the-scenes methodology the Lord gave me and the revelation I received through scriptures. Part Two outlines processes used in my training, along with the various modules to identify your heavenly purpose, map out a blueprint, and develop an executable plan.

I pray that you are filled with the power of the Holy Spirit to know your God-given purpose and assignment and fulfill it to the advancing of God's Kingdom.

"Who has saved us and called us with a holy calling, not according to our works, but according to His own purpose and grace which was given to us in Christ Jesus before time began." 2 Timothy 1:9 NKJV

In Christ's Love,
Brian

PART ONE

1 HOW THIS ALL STARTED

I grew up in Plano, a suburb outside of Dallas, Texas. I would say that it was a normal life, the term *normal* being relative. Growing up in a house with a dad who set high standards and expectations on performance, it was unacceptable to not perform at high levels. If you wanted attention and to spend time with Dad, you learned to perform. I excelled at sports, participated in school projects, was part of my high-school choir and overall walked through the teenage years steadily. I felt great that my merit was based on my level of performance, and I continuously attempted to do more.

My parents divorced when I was sixteen, which was the first of many things that caused my world to shake. It was out of my control and I didn't have the tools or resources at that age to deal with it. So, like most teenagers, I winged it. I built and created habits, patterns, and cycles that were, unknown to me at the time, walls to protect myself from hurt and pain. It was close after the divorce that I rededicated my life to Christ and felt a call to go into ministry. I found that helping and serving others was fulfilling as well as a great buffer to not have to deal with my own personal pain. I became an ultra-performer. I loved sports and basically took that competitive nature inside of me and turned it around to help others. While on the outside it seemed right, correct and admirable; on the inside, I was still creating layers of walls to protect myself from hurt and pain.

Throughout this time I continued to develop a mindset that I was a servant and ministering, but the reality was I continued to run away from anything and anyone that might reveal or resemble my past. I didn't realize then that I was sabotaging my success and my true value as a human being created by God. I was using church and ministry as a crutch to hide me from me. While I achieved some success, I felt like I was always missing the big-ticket item. When were these dreams, desires and visions going to come to pass? I so wanted to hit the mother-load to prove that I was right and that my ways were the ways that the Lord had for me. I left all and completely pursued ministry. I could be found in the church, around the music ministers, hanging out with the pastoral staff and volunteering for anywhere the church had a need. I was there and I prided myself for my dedication and devotion. Intense, yes. I was becoming the ultra-performer. My pattern of the ultra-performer when I was a child growing up had taken on a new look called ministry.

I was a hard-worker, disciplined, studious and committed to the cause of Christ; however, I was completely blinded by the fact I was creating a viscous cycle that was stifling who I was created to be. I attended Rhema Bible Center and Southwestern Assemblies of God University and excelled in my studies. However, in my walk I developed this self-righteous view and a lens that skewed my reality. I was moving farther and farther from what the Lord had for me even amid what I believed was the very center of what He was doing. 'You can be so close and so far, away.'

I left college and got a job with a mortgage company as an assistant loan officer. During my work (which, looking back, was a fantastic experience), I still had this tug in my heart to work in full-time ministry. I didn't understand at the time the pull. I just assumed that it was the Lord and that was what I was called to do. So, in my limited perspective, I left the mortgage industry and moved to a small town in Georgia to serve as a youth pastor for a small church.

Just to note, the Lord is extremely merciful and loves us so much that even while I was in this crazy cycle, I saw the Lord do amazing things in me and in the lives of others. While I was in Georgia, I prayed for a wife. That was the missing piece of my life, so I thought. I was in the ministry, check it off my list. I could help people for the rest of my life, check it off my list. All I needed was a life-partner and we could start a family and serve God. Sounded like bliss. I had it all planned out, just not figured out. I was getting better at keeping myself in my safe zone and didn't realize that the zone was disconnecting me from life. I got married, check it off my list.

7

My ultra-performer personality was growing along with the pride, which I would chalk up to confidence. This is it, now God is going to cause my desires to come to fruition and I will accomplish all that is in my heart. I quickly found out the picture I had in my head of what a Christian marriage looked like was not at all what it was in reality. Hmmm. It had to be the enemy, or my wife, or possibly our geographical location. I was pulling at straws and it never dawned on me I was continuing to drift away and disconnect even more. I ended up going through a divorce after 10 years and three beautiful children. Completely devastated and not knowing how to cope, I reacted again to barricade myself to not feel pain.

I just knew that God didn't want me to be alone so I jumped into another relationship which was my safe place where I could do what the Lord wanted me to do. It never even entered my mind that God wanted me and my heart. I thought that I was surrendered, a student of God's word, and a good person. I have etiquette, manners and a heart who wants to serve others. I turned my experience outward versus taking a long, deep look inside at the possible root causes. The ultra-performer that I became and was continuing to be was alive but not well. Therefore, I need to perform better, be a better servant in my home. This time, marriage was going to be different so I worked and worked so there would be no room for any need. I even was happy with the things that I did, thinking that I was being the gentleman and example of Christ. I felt as if, I had a great grasp on what God wanted to be done and I was on the right trajectory to fulfill this purpose in my life.

I prayed, read the Bible and stayed the course in church. It was the beginning of the same cycle and patterns that I established in my life; the ultra-performer just took on another shape. Several years later, the results began to show. I was more out-of-touch than in touch. I had become too heavenly minded and no earthly good. I would easily dismiss the situations and circumstances I didn't like or want to deal with as a spiritual attack or need for prayer. I spiritualized almost everything and actually thought I was doing a good service. Isn't it interesting that the last person we look at is typically ourselves?

It was not too long after assessing where I was in life that the fruit of my labor was seriously lacking. My dreams remained big but I hadn't progressed the way that I thought I should. Where was the fruit? Was it just supposed to be a longer journey? As time went by more and more questions entered my head, which led me to seek God and His wisdom. Along with my questions, the excuses were right there waiting as well. Using scripture, I could justify anything, including waiting. I wanted to expand my reach and accomplish those huge dreams.

I was out of full-time ministry and left my job to pursue business and life coaching. Wow, what a change. Now, I could really make a difference if I changed the outward appearance. Another lie, but I agreed with it. It was the internal patterns I created from early childhood that still worked on the inside of me, regardless of what they looked like or what they seemed to be on the outside. I later discovered that making the change didn't fix my problems; it only disguised it as the solution.

In a very dark and lonely moment I sat at the dining room table with my head in my hands. I was staring down at a blank piece of paper and begged God to help me put the pieces back together in my life so I could fulfill my purpose. I was lonely, depressed, and cried out to Him. It's times like these the Lord answers in the most comforting way. This is where the ultra-performer turned into a blessing in disguise. I truly desired to get better and see things turn in my life. It was at that time the Lord began the process of opening my eyes to another perspective. I noticed I had a particular frame of reference that was extremely limited and finite. I was in desperate need of a different way to look at this so I could get different results. The Bible states *"And do not be conformed to this world, but be transformed by the renewing of your mind, that you may prove what is that good and acceptable and perfect will of God." Romans 12:2 NKJV* Humbled, I asked God to help me and renew my mind.

"Create in me a clean heart, O God, And renew a steadfast spirit within me. Do not cast me away from Your presence, And do not take Your Holy Spirit from me. Restore to me the joy of Your salvation, And uphold me by Your generous Spirit. Then I will teach transgressors Your ways, And sinners shall be converted to You." Psalm 51:10-13 NKJV

I picked up the pen and began to write out a model that helped me sort through the chaos and confusion I was experiencing. This model mapped out the areas where I thought I really had a handle on, as well as the areas where I knew I needed help. Inspired by the Lord, this motivated me and I started to see areas differently. Individual areas which needed to be evaluated and looked at from an independent perspective as well as from an interdependent perspective. I felt as if I was on the right track. Creativity started to surface. I was inspired and started studying voraciously. I read countless books, listened to audio books and even experienced better results personally. I started speaking about it and helping others walk through the model. They too, experienced great results. The ultra-performer in me was elated and I could see tangible results.

Time passed and my model was intact. I felt I was on the verge of the breakthrough when suddenly my life was turned upside down. My once-healthy marriage was on the rocks and declined rapidly. For various reasons I felt devastated. I found myself back at a place of rebuilding. One of the key rebuilding pieces came when I reconnected with a good friend who would tell me the truth and not sugar coat what he thought I wanted to hear. I was reminded of the scripture *"As iron sharpens iron, so one person sharpens another." Proverbs 27:17 NIV*

The process of getting back on my feet once again was daunting, overwhelming, and many times painful. The only way I knew to get better was to evaluate myself and not make excuses. Throughout this process, I began to notice other people in my life who were brutally honest and others who placated me so I wouldn't be hurt. I chose to go with the tough road, knowing that pain was not my enemy but the indicator I needed freedom. So I set out to seek the truth.

"The pain of the process creates the capacity and wherewithal to hold onto the promise in order to fulfill your purpose." – Brian C. Dobbs

This was the beginning, I decided to develop deeper, more meaningful relationships who challenged me to move forward rather than stay stuck in a rut. I was continuously introspective, wanting to break free from the bondage and make a better life.

I was developing a better me. In all actuality, I was pressing into the person who the Lord created me to be. God looks at us from a finished work and through His guidance we are led to discover who we are in Christ.

What was my passion? Who was I called to? These were constantly circling in my mind and I again went back to my notebook and began to try to make sense of this. It was through situations, circumstances and events that have propelled me forward with a burning desire to see other people set free from the things that are holding them back and walk in the fullness of who the Lord created them to be. To help others know who they are in Christ, what they are called to do and help them fulfill their heavenly calling.

2 CALLING

"For we are His workmanship, created in Christ Jesus for good works, which God prepared beforehand that we should walk in them." Ephesians 2:10 NKJV

Time to regroup. I had a purpose. I understood that God created me for with a purpose and for a particular assignment. The encouraging part was I knew that I could change and continue to improve. Through much prayer and journaling I was brought back to the book of Isaiah, chapter 58 where it talks about being a repairer of the breach. This was one of the first scriptures that stood out to me when I felt the call to go into full-time ministry.

"If you get rid of unfair practices, quit blaming victims, quit gossiping about other people's sins, If you are generous with the hungry and start giving yourselves to the down-and-out, Your lives will begin to glow in the darkness, your shadowed lives will be bathed in sunlight. I will

always show you where to go.
I'll give you a full life in the emptiest of places—firm muscles, strong bones.
You'll be like a well-watered garden, a gurgling spring that never runs dry.
You'll use the old rubble of past lives to build a new, rebuild the foundations from out of your past. You'll be known as those who can fix anything, restore old ruins, rebuild and renovate, make the community livable again." Isaiah 58:9-12 MSG

This passage gave me so much hope. It actually came alive in my spirit and every time that I read it I would see something fresh. This is what I wanted my life to look like. I took this to heart and began to seek the Lord for His guidance. Soon after the Lord led me to a few chapters over to Isaiah 61. Another scripture that inspired me from a very early age.

"The Spirit of the Sovereign Lord is upon me, for the Lord has anointed me to bring good news to the poor, He has sent me to comfort the brokenhearted and to proclaim that captives will be released and prisoners will be freed. He has sent me to tell those who mourn that the time of the Lord's favor has come and with it, the day of God's anger against their enemies. To all who mourn in Israel, he will give a crown of beauty for ashes, a joyous blessing instead of mourning, festive praise instead of despair. In their righteousness, they will be like great oaks that the Lord has planted for his own glory. They will rebuild the ancient ruins, repairing cities destroyed long ago. They will revive them, though they have been deserted for many generations." Isaiah

61:1-4 NLT

It was the beginning where the Lord opened my

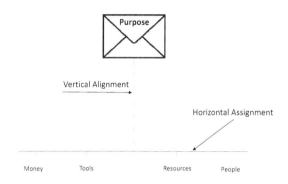

eyes to the scriptures in an illustrated way to see what this meant in pictures. So I began to draw. I was a visual learner and I could see the envelope with the alignment and assignment. From this illustration I knew it was my job to discover what was inside of the envelope. It was my purpose. And when I unlocked the vertical piece, then the horizontal piece would begin to make sense.

I believe we all have a God-given purpose inside of us. Throughout the scriptures we see people accepting God's plans for their lives and accomplishing great exploits.

"The people who know their God shall be strong, and carry out great exploits." Daniel 11:32b NKJV

I discovered most of what I was seeking was not actually purpose at all, but fell in a responsibility or a luxury category. Neither one was bad; however, for the sake of my life's purpose I noticed a common denominator with both categories. They were variables. The current responsibilities and what I deemed as luxury both had timelines associated with them. For example, what I thought was fun, exciting and luxurious in my twenties was not the case when I turned forty. On the responsibility side, I noticed how raising my children changed from when they were infants to when they were in high school. I came to realize that even if I never acquired anything from relationships to interests, the Lord still gave me a purpose.

"Before I formed you in the womb I knew you; before you were born I set you apart; I appointed you as a prophet to the nations." Jeremiah 1:5 NIV

So, the quest began. I wrote down an interesting question to myself. If I had all the time and money I needed, what would I find myself doing? I knew I would need the capital to finance the vision as well as the freedom of time to accomplish the vision. After all, I noticed my past jobs were a means to make money so I could spend my time doing what I loved. Plus, having time with no money wasn't a great place to be and having money with no time was not appealing either.

This question led me to a flood of thoughts that came from every direction. Did I want a new car, home, travel, minister, help the homeless and more? Actually the thoughts kept me spinning. Going back to the original question, *if I had financial independence and freedom of time, what would I find myself doing?* This question wasn't complete. So, I added a phrase to the question: *If I had all the money and time and I had to contribute back to society or mankind what would it be?*

Initially I wanted to preach. Now it was not just preaching, but I specifically wanted to see people set free to do what God has called them to do.

"My people are destroyed for lack of knowledge". Hosea 4:6 NKJV

I could clearly see that God has called me and anointed me. Now what? I didn't really know how or where to start. Along with most things I did what I thought was the best. As I mentioned earlier, I went to Bible college, studied scripture and served in the church. The major component I lacked was a clear vision; not necessarily of the finished project, but I needed a better road map to get me from one phase to the next and see the progress (if any) that I was making.

It is one thing to have a vision of the macro but it is another to be able to process both the macro and micro together. I desired to see the large picture with the next steps phases and steps to begin moving in the right direction. However, every time that I would look at the purpose I would get excited and then get stuck because it was too overwhelming.

At that time, I wasn't able to break it down into manageable sections. Plus, the nagging voice inside my head that would tell me if you figured it out then it wasn't faith. I believe that our Heavenly Father is so interested in the outcome that He becomes super involved in the process.

"If any of you lacks wisdom, let him ask of God, who gives to all liberally and without reproach, and it will be given to him." James 1:5 NKJV

The first illustration I drew had columns, the envelope was my purpose and it was my responsibility to follow the clues that God set before me to find. As I started asking the Lord, I knew that there were some pieces that I would need to bring this into fruition. Suddenly, I discovered all three columns in my illustration. Two columns, luxury and responsibilities, were variables. These have seasons or time stamps on them. The middle column was the constant which was purpose. The Bible says we know in part and prophesy in part; so knowing everything about your purpose immediately was not going to happen. It looks like it evolves but I am more convinced now that as we continue to seek God and His will for our lives, we move closer to understanding His
purpose with all the different facets.

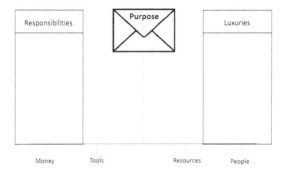

I started asking God for insights, ideas and concepts. Next steps and strategies. As I continued to seek the Lord, I found that revelations and downloads would come as if they dropped down from heaven to me. Each light bulb moment was exciting; however, a lot of time only a piece of the puzzle and not the whole puzzle. I have also discovered that the Father enjoys it when His children seek Him for guidance and counsel.

"Call to Me, and I will answer you, and show you great and mighty things, which you do not know." Jeremiah 33:3 NKJV

I began to collect puzzle pieces from my time with the Lord. At times I would think that I got the missing or final piece but realized that it was just a piece. I began to create a list of items needed to accomplish the assignment. It was going to take money to fulfill the vision, yes, but where was I going to get this and how much would it cost exactly? The second item I knew I would need were people and connections. Where were they, and if I didn't have the amount of money I needed, then how could I hire people for free? The third item was tools. With a technologically advanced society I could think of hundreds of items needed including web presence, digital footprints, collateral and much more. The fourth item I needed was resources. Did I have the network, libraries and structure to necessary to grow, sustain and scale? Even with unanswered questions I kept moving forward.

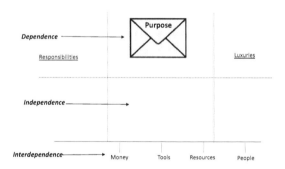

This process brought up three additional areas in this illustration I knew I needed:

1. <u>Dependence.</u> Since God put this in my heart then I knew it was up to Him to bring it to pass. I had to become completely dependent on God and

believe His word. Hold on to His promises because they are yes and amen. I knew it would require a deeper commitment and surrender to the Lord as I walked this journey out. It was my responsibility to stay in tune with God's word and become obedient to follow His guidance. I spent time in His word, worshipping not only on Sundays but throughout the week. I set my mind to draw closer to God.

"Be diligent to present yourself approved to God, a worker who does not need to be ashamed, rightly dividing the word of truth." 2 Timothy 2:15 NKJV

2. Independence. This is the one that somehow was misplaced. I had to come to a healthy understanding that nobody was going to make me successful or do it for me. I had a part and was responsible for my actions, thoughts, behaviors and so on. I had to take responsibility to study and do my part while being completely yielded to the Lord. I was not opposed to outside accountability, actually liked it. The bottom line was that whether I had people there or not I was still one hundred percent responsible for my activities and choices. This is the place where I developed disciplines to keep me on track. I needed systems and a routine that I could stay on course. No more excuses.

"And in him you too are being built together to become a dwelling in which God lives by his Spirit." Eph 2:22 NIV

3. <u>Interdependence</u> was the third piece that I found in this equation. I had always desired to work with a team of people who loved the Lord, were passionate like I was and shared a unified vision. Although, being burned numerous times I never gave up on the team idea. Going through various challenges created in me the ability to break out of barriers and create boundaries which has enabled me to navigate the course. It is in the community that I received additional encouragement and wisdom. I remained opened to surrounding myself with good people.

"Above all else, guard your heart, for everything you do flows from it." Proverbs 4:23 NIV

The interdependence was not only related to people but also my relationship with money, tools and resources. They are necessary and God gives us everything that we need for life and godliness. The trick was not becoming codependent and allowing these to become idols in my life.

I needed more answers. The road map I asked for was terrific; but even with the course having being set, I had to know where I was in all of this. The Lord began to answer my prayers for help and change. He became my coach, and led me through the scriptures.

.

3 WHERE AM I?

"Jesus said to him, 'You shall love the Lord your God with all your heart, with all your soul, and with all your mind.' This is the first and great commandment. And the second is like it: 'You shall love your neighbor as yourself.' On these two commandments hang all the Law and the Prophets." Matthew 22:37-39 NKJV

As I mentioned earlier, the Lord gifted me with the ability to see and map out the scripture into a visual illustration; so with this passage, I began to draw and create the various modules and systems to help assess the different areas of life.

The moment at the dining room table really motivated me to get connected back to my life in all areas. Accomplishing and reconnecting would take the ability to see what I was working with, so I created an eight-chart table. I wanted to stop this vicious cycle of chaos and confusion, just going through life in survival mode. It was time to thrive. It was time to take personal responsibility for my life. I would often say, you can spend all your time containing chaos or you can compartmentalize to manage effectively; but I had to apply – really apply it – to my own life. I wrote down the areas where I wanted to be present and connect. From that exercise, eight areas emerged as subsystems of everyday life so I could determine my perceived level of connectivity. I envisioned this table as a battery pack. Compartmentalizing the eight cells shows how if one cell is empty, then the other cells would have to compensate for the lack in any one given cell. Plus, it gave me a great indicator of how much energy I was operating at any given time in my life. I could see what areas needed immediate attention and what areas could be affected by concentrating on different activities.

Where   your   focus   goes   your   power   flows.

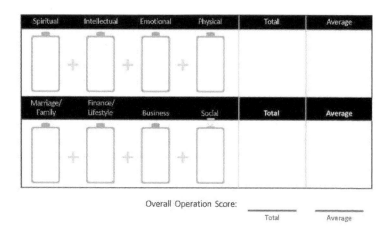

Spiritual	Intellectual	Emotional	Physical	Total	Average

Marriage/ Family	Finance/ Lifestyle	Business	Social	Total	Average

Overall Operation Score:

Total   Average

I didn't tackle all eight at the same time, which didn't seem healthy or possible. So, I separated the eight cells into Internal and External. Through evaluating my life according to these eight areas I discovered a way to really dive deep to define the what, how, and why each area's role played out in my life.

Once I developed the areas, I wanted something to reflect an independent and interdependent model to show a single item and the overall impact it has on the whole. Too many times, in my personal life and working with others, there has been a tendency to make a mountain out of one single area. When you focus all the attention on that one area, it begins to spin out of control. This is often followed by "My whole life is horrible;" when the fact of the matter is, certain areas could have a significant overall impact if addressed individually.

The Bible says, *"for as he thinks in his heart, so is he." Proverbs 23:7 NLT.* This life principle applies to how you or I view ourselves in any one of these areas and the whole. I learned personal development is not merely getting the results that you want as much as it is learning personal responsibility and ownership.

Now that the model was developed, separated into eight cells, four internal and four external, I had something to work with. Given that each cell is independent and has an overall interdependence, the cell makes up a part of our lives and the responsibility lies within each of us to make sure each area is strong.

This brought me to another major point in this process. I had the model and now I needed good metrics to score myself. Also, with a good metric system I could measure personal growth. My perception is my reality, and with that I scored myself from a holistic way. I wasn't a fan of the 1-10 scoring model I had grown accustomed to throughout life, so I decided to go with another scoring system.

I took a zero to 90 scale, with 90 being an A, 80 to 89 was a B, 70 to 79 was a C, 60 to 69 was a D and so on. This provoked more thought and caused me to look at each cell with the ability to make a passing score of 60 up to 90 or failing score less than 60.

It was interesting to discover that generating a 90 in each of the top four cells equals 360 – which revealed another truth that helped me progress. There are 360 degrees in a circle, which represents the finite aspect. The infinite aspect of a circle is the number of points in it. If you take care of your side of the circle, you open yourself up to infinite possibilities and opportunities. We as humans are finite and God, being infinite, reiterated the importance of being completely dependent and independent as I developed.

Measuring each cell on a 0-90 scale was the first step to see how much I would score myself in each area. The interdependence showed itself when I took the total of each cell and then divided by four to get the internal score, then added up the four external cells to get the average on the external side. I then took both averages, added them together and divided by two to see my life score.

Creating this exercise was one thing, it was not until I took a real good look at this worksheet did it all soak in. I felt life was caving in and it seemed as if I could not stop spiraling out of control. I began writing my scores down in each area personally. Just taking a step to make progress provided a temporary relief. I analyzed each area and scored myself on the way I felt that I was functioning in that area. At the end I tallied up my scores and wrote down my average. Wow. This was truth telling and suddenly my temporary relief was nowhere to be found. To tackle every area wasn't feasible nor did I have the bandwidth at that moment. I had to choose. I picked the three areas that would give me the best hopes to stop spiraling. I chose spiritual, family and finances and that is where I began. I picked three and started writing action items that I could accomplish each day to better my score. I continued to work through the process and eventually saw improvements. There was light at the end of the tunnel. When I got to a point where the scores increased I went back to the scorecard and added two additional areas to improve. Still staying focused on the first three it was easier to incorporate the next two areas. I became ultra-intentional and deliberate because I wanted to see true change. The entire process of working through each area took time but it was completely worth it. I saw growth and change take place. How I handled situations in the past was completely different to how I was handling them now. I was happier, healthier and my relationships were better.

Wow, this was groundbreaking and it became a lifestyle not merely a one and done event. Now I could see where I was, what I could work on immediately to boost my score, and I knew my score wasn't finality. The score could fluctuate. This gave me hope I could always look at my score and take the appropriate actions to continue to improve. I could manage life since I had a clearer picture on compartmentalizing versus having a skewed vision where everything was overlapping and convoluted.

Principle One: Connectivity

You have heard the old saying *the chain is only as strong as the weakest link.* Also, when you think about the physiological makeup of our bodies, we can understand that when a part is hurt, broken or disabled, the other parts of the body have to overcompensate in order to make up the difference.

So, when I looked at this assessment I could conceptualize a top level of battery cells and a bottom level of battery cells. I designed it this way to show a compartmentalized system that is interdependent on each of the other cells. This means that no one cell is above the other; they all have their place and play a unique role throughout the course of our lives.

"He makes the whole body fit together perfectly. As each part does its own special work, it helps the other parts grow, so that the whole body is healthy and growing and full of love." Ephesians 4:16 NLT

Principle Two: Internal and External

The top row of battery cells helps to understand the internal side of the equation. The bottom row represents the external side of the equation. The top row consists of areas in our lives where we are solely responsible, such as our spiritual, emotional, intellectual and physical state. This is what we came into the world with. Our spirit, mind and body.

The bottom row of the battery cells helps to understand how we function and operate with others as well as getting the desired results in quality of life through our relationships, finances and business. These areas are acquired as we go through life, such as relationships, careers and financial lifestyles.

Principle Three: Measurements

This piece is specifically designed to give a total average and individual averages in order to be able to become more strategic in bringing up your score in one area or overall score on life. The scoring system is based on a 0-90 point system. I am a firm believer in metrics. It is nearly impossible to measure what you don't count. Surrounded by numbers almost every day, it was easy for me to assign a number to how I perceived an area to be.

Principle Four: Infinite and Finite

The model has four battery cells on the top row and four battery cells on the bottom row. If you score 90 points in each of the cells on the top, you have 360 total points for an optimal score. There are 360 degrees in a circle so our job is to make sure we optimize our circle. There are an infinite amount of points in a circle as well. So, regardless of how hard we work at improving, growing and striving for more, no one is perfect. We factor in the infinite because, with all of our hard work and striving for excellence, we can be comforted that there are infinite possibilities that will and can come into our circles to assist us on our journeys.

Principle Five: New Beginnings

Eight denotes a new beginning or a new first. This assessment, which reveals our life score, has identified eight battery cells, or domains, representing the major areas from a compartmentalized and overall state of being. When you can take the 30,000-foot snapshot and then dive into each area like a surgeon, you can have hope restored, knowing you have an opportunity for a new beginning in life no matter where you are currently or what stage of life you are in. Next, I began to write about the domains as how I saw life's operating system.

"Love the Lord with all of your heart." in Matthew 22:37 NKJV seemed like an ideal starting point. This was the spiritual area. My walk with the Lord started when I was young. I accepted Jesus as Lord in my life and was baptized at the age of 10. When I was 16, I felt the desire to go into full-time ministry. So the spiritual domain came very natural to me. I loved God and wanted to serve Him. It makes sense that this was the first of the eight, as I wanted to make sure I was present, connected and doing my part. Was I growing in my relationship with God? Was I reading the Bible and spending time in prayer? Was I connected to the church? Was I doing what the Lord desired for me to do in my life? These were some of the questions that I asked myself to see if and how I could score myself in this

area.

"Love the Lord with all of your soul" Matthew 22:37 NKJV was the second area in this system. I understood that the soul could be divided into the ability to reason, which I called the intellectual domain; and the capacity to feel, which I categorized as the emotional domain.

Intellectual. The intellectual side of us is that capacity to reason and comprehend. It seats the human will and is where choices are made. How was I progressing intellectually? Was I getting smarter, gaining wisdom and understanding? The scriptures tell us in Proverbs 4:7 NKJV *"Wisdom is the principal thing; Therefore get wisdom and in all your getting, get understanding."* I knew I had to be coachable and become a life-long learner, and I was grateful for that. What did I want to learn more about? Was I reading enough and what was I reading about? Was I able to speak intelligently on different subjects? Who and what was I listening to? As I was going through this exercise my mind was flooded with thoughts.

Emotional. The other part of the soul realm was the emotional capacity we have as humans. This aspect of life is where we feel and exercise our five senses. Once I got to the emotional part, I started to search out what the Bible said about emotions and was this a valid part of this assessment? The Lord led me to many scriptures that validated this was an important area to have. *"The joy of the Lord is our strength,"* which is found in Nehemiah 8:10 NKJV. Plus, I looked at the fruit of the spirit, which is love, joy, peace, patience, kindness, goodness, gentleness, faithfulness and self-control. I could see how emotions played a large roll in this. Many times we are asked by people who love us how we are feeling. The extremes of our emotions are not only noticeable but unhealthy. There are those who choose not to feel while others are completely driven by emotions. I wanted to have a healthy balance emotionally.

Physical. *"Love the Lord with all of your strength."* Matthew 22:37 NKJV I could relate to the physical area. The physical aspect comprises our overall health in a physical well-being. I wanted to make sure that I was doing my part to keep my body healthy. I realized if I wanted to serve the Lord and finish the work that He called me to, then I needed to have the physical strength and capability to do the work. The body is the temple of the Holy Spirit. *"Or do you not know that your body is the temple of the Holy Spirit who is in you, whom you have from God, and you are not your own?" 1 Corinthians 6:19 NKJV* If my body is the temple of the Holy Spirit, then was I taking care of it properly? Was I eating healthy foods? Did I have a good workout routine? Was I getting the proper amount of sleep? I couldn't just live life and assume that I was healthy as long as I was not experiencing sickness or pain. I wanted to take a proactive stance and be a good steward of what I was given. I committed not to take for granted my health and well-being.

Marriage/Family. *"He who finds a wife finds a good*

thing, And obtains favor from the Lord." Proverbs 18:22 NKJV and, *"Behold, children are a heritage from the Lord, the fruit of the womb is a reward." Psalm 127:3 NKJV*

This was a place where I placed such a high value, and still do. Was I living the way the Lord wanted me to live, being the head of my household and a great husband? As a parent, was I taking time to be present with my wife and children? Was I cultivating healthy communication habits that would build the family unit? These were extremely important to me. Now I just needed to study to know how to do my part. We can't control other people but that doesn't make it right to abdicate our responsibility. Was I spending quality time? Was I effectively communicating with my wife, children and family? Was I becoming a better listener?

Financial and Lifestyle. *"And you shall remember the Lord your God, for it is He who gives you the power to get wealth, that He may establish His covenant which He swore to your fathers, as it is this day." Deuteronomy 8:18 NKJV* This area was a major component in this assessment. I knew that it took finances to live as well as accomplish all that I had in my heart to do. The lifestyle we create is to ultimately bring glory back to God. So with that, I began my quest to learn more about finances and building wealth. I couldn't go with the status quo any longer if I desired to get ahead. I had to do something for things to change and improve. Money has its place and I needed to gain the wisdom and knowledge to know how to make money work for me, versus me working for money in order to showcase the lifestyle that brought glory to God. How was I handling debt? Was I saving and investing wisely? Did I have a plan to learn and grow? Was I getting counsel from the right group of people? If people looked at my lifestyle, would it direct their attention back to God?

Business. *"This Book of the Law shall not depart from your mouth, but you shall meditate in it day and night, that you may observe to do according to all that is written in it. For then you will make your way prosperous, and then you will have good success."* *Joshua 1:8 NKJV* This area showed me how I was contributing back as well as how I spent my time earning a living. Did I choose a career or was it my calling? I was caught in such a quandary for a good part of my life due to being pulled from different sides. I wanted to serve the Lord in my calling and I needed to earn money to survive. I had to develop a new lens which completely led to my freedom. I began to see business as a way for me to improve who I was personally, make the world around me a little better every day, and as a vehicle to generate an overflow for my overall purpose. Work wasn't outside of my calling anymore, it became Kingdom business.

Social. *"Therefore encourage one another and build each other up, just as in fact you are doing."* *1 Thessalonians 5:11 NIV* This area can be challenging as well. How do you measure who is in your circle, and what are you supposed to do with that? As I dove into this area I began to understand the importance of being equally yoked to the community where I placed myself. Were they going where I wanted to go? Did they share similar passions or interests in advancing God's kingdom? I had to ask myself these tough questions and be okay with the answers I found. It was then when I came across a quote, *You are the average of the top five people you hang out with the most*, that was an eye opener. This didn't mean to be tacky or hateful to people. It wasn't an excuse to not be Christlike and love people unconditionally. It meant that the people with whom I could be transparent with and receive the wisdom they were giving had be going in the same direction the Lord was taking me.

All these were puzzle pieces. I noticed the energy spikes as I pressed through the process. It was like a scavenger hunt, only in real life. Each puzzle piece looked crystal clear and gave me the sensation that this was it, later to find out that the crooked edges of the puzzle piece had some missing sides to make it whole. The blessing in all of this was the insight I received, and it continued to build upon itself. God's word says that He teaches us line upon line and precept upon precept. *"For precept must be upon precept, precept upon precept, Line upon line, line upon line, Here a little, there a little." Isaiah 28:10 NKJV* I knew when He was encouraging me to press forward, regardless of my situation and circumstances.

Through these events, the Lord brought me back to the model I was so excited about. My understanding broadened and I could see the harmony inside the model that made it come alive.

4 EIGHT STAGES OF TRANSFORMATION

"This means that anyone who belongs to Christ has become a new person. The old life is gone; a new life has begun!" 2 Corinthians 5:17 NLT

The next step after regrouping was to map out a plan that led to transformation. I wanted to know the stages to go through to accomplish transformation. As the Lord led me to the scriptures, I realized the Word, being the seed, could be applied to multiple areas.

"Being confident of this very thing, that He who has begun a good work in you will complete it until the day of Jesus Christ" Philippians 1:6 NKJV

Throughout this journey, I have grown keenly aware of how my thoughts, feelings and actions need to be grounded in the truth. It is the truth makes us free, keeps us free and moving in the right direction. I am fully convinced that if your heart is genuinely seeking out the truth, then God in His infinite ability will keep rerouting your steps until you get to your desired destination.

Could the results overshadow your need for personal responsibility? I could very easily see that if the Lord had answered my prayers and given me the success that I was looking for at that time, then I wouldn't have seen the need to grow or develop in that area or other areas.

How does this process work? I began to study the parable of the sower, and it became alive to me:

"Listen! A farmer went out to plant some seeds. As he scattered them across his field, some seeds fell on a footpath, and the birds came and ate them. Other seeds fell on shallow soil with underlying rock. The seeds sprouted quickly because the soil was shallow. But the plants soon wilted under the hot sun, and since they didn't have deep roots, they died. Other seeds fell among thorns that grew up and choked out the tender plants. Still other seeds fell on fertile soil, and they produced a crop that was thirty, sixty, and even a hundred times as much as had been planted! Anyone with ears to hear should listen and understand." Matthew 13: 3-9; 18-23 NKJV

Here's the explanation of the parable about the farmer planting seeds: The seed that fell on the footpath represents those who hear the message about the Kingdom and don't understand it. Then the evil one comes and snatches away the seed that was planted in their hearts. The seed on the rocky soil represents those who hear the message and immediately receive it with joy. But since they don't have deep roots, they don't last long. They fall away as soon as they have problems or are persecuted for believing God's word. The seed that fell among the thorns represents those who hear God's word, but all too quickly the message is crowded out by the worries of this life and the lure of wealth, so no fruit is produced. The seed that fell on good soil represents those who truly hear and understand God's word and produce a harvest of thirty, sixty, or even a hundred times as much as had been planted.

With that, I continued to develop a personal desire for structure and systems in my life. No longer did I want to leave things to chance. Yes, I knew I needed to live by faith and I also knew the scripture says faith without works are dead. *"But do you want to know, O foolish man, that faith without works is dead?" James 2:20 NKJV.* It dawned on me when I could map out the transformation process, I could see where I was and what needed to happen to get me to the next step.

Stage 1 – Know it All

When the seed fell on the hard soil, the birds came and stole the seed. I needed a fresh perspective and had to admit that I didn't know it all. Plus, I had to be willing to change. I had to humble myself in the sight of the Lord and He would lift me up. I checked my knowledge in at the door and proceeded to ask the Lord to give me understanding. If I was going to change any area I couldn't rely on my past knowledge or experience to get me to where I have never been before. The new level requires a new perspective and new knowledge base.

Stage 2 – Idea Zone

What did the scripture mean when it talked about the seed sprouting up in the rocky soil, and when the sun came up it was scorched because it had no roots? The revelation I received in this stage was exciting. It was the stage that you could get that million-dollar idea or the next step to your adventure. It was when the light bulb goes on. However, it was more like a flash in the pan. There were no roots to sustain growth. There was work to do. I had to remove some rocks, which meant I needed to map out a plan and remove as many obstacles and hindrances in my way to get this off the ground. This is where more research and data was required to substantiate true and lasting change. Staying disciplined was key to making progress.

Stage 3 – Noise Zone

The weeds choke the seed out. This is where I knew I needed to get extremely focused and be discerning from the naysayers around me including all self-talk in my head. I would need to have the map and structure laid out so I could be consistent in doing the tasks that would bring me closer to my goals. I couldn't be distracted by the cares of this world because they would choke out the seed. Plus, in this stage I understood the importance to block out all negativity and fear in accomplishing the tasks. *"For God has not given us a spirit of fear, but of power and of love and of a sound mind." 2 Timothy 1:7 NKJV.* I was determined to stay focused and committed.

Stage 4 – Foundation

The good soil. In order to get into the good soil and have the best opportunity for success there were areas that needed to be torn down, habits uprooted and systems overhauled. The Bible says we are to renounce the hidden things of shame. *"But we have renounced the hidden things of shame, not walking in craftiness nor handling the word of God deceitfully, but by manifestation of the truth commending ourselves to every man's conscience in the sight of God." 2 Corinthians 4:2 NKJV.* Renounce means to completely disown them. No more unforgiveness, resentment, jealousy or bitterness allowed. No more excuses. I was taking complete ownership of my goal and was committed to see it through. This has now become my responsibility and with the help of the Lord I could get rid of the things holding me back and move forward. "I can do all things through Christ who strengthens me." Philippians 4:13 NKJV

Stage 5 – Foundation 2.0

The second part in the good soil was to go deep and expand on each side. Expand my knowledge, my strength, and capacity to accomplish more. This is not an easy phase but it was definitely rewarding as I began to realize I was getting stronger. This was the time to start building on the foundation the Lord gave me. This was the time to begin to plant and expect a bountiful harvest. The pain of the process was creating in me the capacity to carry the promise and fulfill my God-given calling. I sought the Lord more and looked for wisdom. I wanted the change and set my sights on obtaining the prize. I spoke the Lord's word over me and the process.

Stage 6 – Revelation

Little by little I was able to make progress. I noticed the things of the past which would knock me off course or derail me were not effective as they were before the process. I began to see how my thoughts changed and I was not as volatile as before. I could stand my ground, knowing the promise that He put into my heart was becoming a reality. It was like going to the gym and lifting weights. In the beginning it was challenging but I could lift a few times. The more I lifted, the easier it became. The internal strength is what I noticed. It was the ability to persevere and overcome. *"But thanks be to God, who gives us the victory through our Lord Jesus Christ."* 1 *Corinthians 15:57 NKJV*. On the outside I didn't notice much change, but on the inside there was something really happening. My mind was also being enlightened more often.

Stage 7 – Manifestation

The more I dove into this process the more excited I became. God takes us from faith to faith and from glory to glory. I was beginning to see more clearly and was able to hear what the Lord was asking me to do. Things were taking shape on the outside as well because I was in alignment to the assignment that the Lord has given to me. It was evident in my walk that something was changing and I was even being told by others they have noticed something different about me. I saw results from my work, finances, speaking and more progress in areas of my life where I worked so long behind the scenes. I even saw improvement in the normal every day activities. This was great news. I was beginning to see the fruits of my labor. Changes were taking place and I wanted to keep going to see it come to fruition.

Stage 8 – Transformation

Some produce 30 fold, 60 fold and 100 fold return. I'm in a new place and I am thrilled. The process I went through was a total metamorphosis and the results looked nothing like the beginning condition; no different than the tree looking different from the seed or the butterfly looking different from the caterpillar. I saw things differently. Heard things differently. Did things differently. Why? Because I went through the process and was different. I didn't wait for things to change around me to become different. I chose to do things differently which caused things to change around me. What I had inside of me completely transformed my life to be the person God called me to be. I had to surrender to Him and to the process, doing my part as well as owning up to my responsibilities.

EIGHT STAGES OF TRANSFORMATION

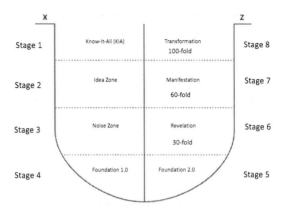

5 TIME TO TAKE ACTION

"Arise, for this matter is your responsibility . We also are with you. Be of good courage, and do it." Ezra 10:4 NKJV

"Now is the time," I said. I didn't want to delay the results any longer than necessary. I went back and got my scorecard, identified the three lowest scores and came up with some action items I could implement that would make a difference. I knew that if I could create a regimen to follow, I could determine if I was making progress to get the results that I desired to see. The key was not to quit and even when I was stuck, tired or lacked motivation, the Lord would bring someone or something across my path that would spark the fire once again.

Just a quick note on failure to start. Failing to start something or not knowing where to start is based out of fear. Fear leaves us paralyzed and stagnated. *"Fear not, for I am with you; Be not dismayed, for I am your God. I will strengthen you, Yes, I will help you, I will uphold you with My righteous right hand." Isaiah 41:10 NKJV*

So, starting anywhere was at least a step in the right direction. Another tip is that I didn't have to accomplish everything at once. This brought me freedom and a sense of hope that I could tackle one area at a time and maintain significant progress. I picked out steps that were attainable and I could do them consistently over a long period of time. It took me a little while to understand that small steps weren't insignificant; it was the steps done over a long period of time that would create a compounding effect.

I monitored my score and would add tasks into my daily routine as I saw fit; meaning, nothing had to be overwhelming to make a difference. Once I mastered or set up steps in one or two areas, I could then add more steps and even more areas because I created a larger bandwidth for the tasks. Plus, the more you do something the easier the task becomes and then you are able to make additions.

This gave me a greater sense of accomplishment. I was moving, and moving in the right direction. No longer stagnated, I had a game plan and I was responsible for the actions, and I could see the results happen directly in proportion to my activities. I got out of the habit of chasing results and got into the mindset of creating the right plan and activities which produced the results I desired. Another phrase of mine is, stop chasing the things that are meant to follow.

Create the Path

The path is an interesting system that I stumbled

across that has helped accelerate the process. As humans, are brains are naturally wired to take the path of least resistance. So, to accelerate the process I began to think through and draw out every detail of the path I needed to take to accomplish the task. For example, the night before, I set my coffee maker to go off at the same time every morning and have my gym clothes picked out; so once I finish my morning devotional and reading, I can head to the gym. This was a consistent pattern and easy path to follow once established.

Walking on a path is typically easier than trying to find your way through the woods without one. I applied the same principle to each area and even was able to combine areas with activities that would benefit multiple areas. For example, my morning routine mentioned above included my spiritual walk with the Lord by reading my devotion in the morning, the professional or personal development book that I include in my morning routine added value to sharpening my skills as a professional, and my time at the gym after my reading kept me in physical shape. The emotional area also benefited through working out, reading and staying consistent with my daily routine.

The success I generated kept me going and I began to make better paths for other areas. I took time prior to launching a new project to forecast everything I would need before, during and after the task. The better the path the faster I could get results. Once I got my path where I thought it needed to be, I launched. After the launch I remained conscientious about the path and made adjustments as needed. The first few times no adjustments were made, just an observation. I knew if something was working, don't break it. The path was not set in stone again giving me the freedom to change when necessary. However, keeping the focus on the goal was still there.

Establish a Rhythm

I stayed with the regimen and kept doing it, day after day. What I found in the process is this structure was easy to follow, and it kept getting better and better results. I naturally progressed and the things that I listed got easier, and the easier they became the faster I could accomplish them. In the levels of competency, I was now moving into the level of conscious competence. This level is where you know how and what to do, and with practice you become better. Repetition was key in this part of my process.

Finding the balance in the action steps created a rhythm in my day which caused better results. This part of my day was and continues to be very protected because the time was working for me and not against me. Plus, when I deviated from the plan for whatever reason I could easily go back to the path and regain momentum. I found my stride, developed a rhythm and saw true life changing results.

"The diligent find freedom in their work; the lazy are oppressed by work."   *Proverbs*   *12:24*   *MSG*

Expanding God's Kingdom on the inside of me had to happen first in order for me to become more effective in expanding His Kingdom on the outside.

Creating the path as well as the rhythm led me to be more conscientious of my thoughts, feelings and actions. Along with creating the regimen that I could follow I also had to keep my thoughts and feelings in check too.

Step 1: Thoughts

"Casting down arguments and every high thing that exalts itself against the knowledge of God, bringing every thought into captivity to the obedience of Christ" 2 Corinthians 10:5

If you are not conscientious about where you are and what you are doing, it is going to be difficult and merely impossible to change. I had to take control of my thoughts and not just let things pass through my brain without being checked out first. It was a step in the right direction. A step that required me being present and not passively approaching life.

What were the things affecting my thoughts? Romans 12:2 *NKJV* says *"We are transformed by the renewing of our minds."* That was the first clue to me that if I am transformed, then I can be transformed into something that I don't want to be equally as much.

I looked at the things I was letting into my thought life and the area of visualization. What was I constantly looking at, watching and paying attention to? I had to be intentional on the items I was going to spend time watching. This made a difference in a short amount of time.

The other area which needed monitoring was what I was listening to. The Bible also says *"Faith comes by hearing and hearing by the word of God." Romans 10:17 NKJV* The opposite is true as well, meaning that what I listened to the most was where my faith or belief system would be strengthened. So, I put an end to listening to most media until I could build a good filtering system to protect my thoughts.

The only thing left to monitor came down to the thought life that I had prior to making these initiatives to change. This was the internal process, yet it seemed difficult at the time because I had to overcome negative self-talk. One of the primary ways was to feed my thoughts with positive and motivating messages. Additionally, I found strength in speaking what I wanted, daily affirmations and positive self-talk.

"Death and life are in the power of the tongue, and those who love it will eat its fruit." Proverbs 18:21

My thought life improved. My communication to myself improved. I became present and aware of my thoughts and I could see a direct correlation to the results I was seeing.

Step 2: Feelings

"How do I control my feelings?" was the question I had. I wanted to be proactive versus reactive and all I could think of is how feelings, for the most part at that time in my life, were reactive. Did they have to be? The answer is No. My feelings of happiness, anger, sadness, peace could still be there but I could be in charge. There is a time to feel and that was important to me not to become so robotic that I lost touch with human feelings. This is a way people connect and relate to each other. I asked the Lord to show me and he began to minister to me in a very soft and loving way like a parent to a child.

"These things I have spoken to you, that My joy may remain in you, and that your joy may be full." John 15:11 NKJV

Joy was a feeling and it was a strength. This brought a lot of thoughts concerning joy.

"Be anxious for nothing, but in everything by prayer and supplication, with thanksgiving, let your requests be made known to God; and the peace of God, which surpasses all understanding, will guard your hearts and minds through Christ Jesus." Philippians 4:6-7 NKJV

Peace was a feeling and it was a guard or protector. Studying these two verses with several others, I began to create a filtering system for my emotions. Do I have peace and joy in this situation, circumstance, relationship or activity? Waiting a few seconds before I made my decision led me to become more proactive in my emotions and not be run by them. I was in control and the Lord who lives inside of me was my counselor.

Step 3: Actions
"But without faith it is impossible to please Him, for he who comes to God must believe that He is, and that He is a rewarder of those who diligently seek Him." Hebrews 11:6 NKJV

Since, it is impossible to please God without faith. I created the path and rhythm from what I desired to see and now it was time to mix my actions with my new formed thought and feeling process.

Did I really believe I could receive the things I was looking for? I am a student of God's Word and understood prayer and the power of it. I was especially good at believing for other peoples' miracles and successes. Now it was time to start believing the same for my stuff as I believed for others.

No more action without a supercharged belief and the right thought boundaries. This practice made me evaluate the steps before I took them. Yes, taking a leap of faith is one thing. Taking a leap of faith with your thoughts aligned and your feelings in check creates amazing results. I knew the Lord would teach me to mold the three actions, feelings and thoughts into one cord which carries a huge amount of strength.

Then Jesus said to the disciples, "Have faith in God. I tell you the truth, you can say to this mountain, 'May you be lifted up and thrown into the sea,' and it will happen. But you must really believe it will happen and have no doubt in your heart. I tell you, you can pray for anything, and if you believe that you've received it, it will be yours." Mark 11:22-24 NLT

The more I remained consistent to create a path and a rhythm while being conscientious about my thoughts, feelings and actions I produced results I was looking for. I wasn't perfect in the beginning and haven't reached perfection yet; however, the growth I have seen in my life from the feelings, thoughts, actions along with the ability to accomplish things has been substantial. The more I learned the more excited I became. Each step was important and continued to build upon each other as I pass from one season to the next with the Lord.

6 MY BRAND

"I thank you, God, for making me so mysteriously complex! Everything you do is marvelously breathtaking. It simply amazes me to think about it! How thoroughly you know me, Lord!" Psalms 139:14 TPT

I discovered a deeper and more meaningful way of life. I was discovering who I was. It was interesting that as I surrendered to the process, I became in tune with God and life again. No longer did I want to be dissociated in life just going through the motions. It was amazing the clarity and focus I had gained and I continued to press into the Lord. The Bible says *"All praise to God, the Father of our Lord Jesus Christ, who has blessed us with every spiritual blessing in the heavenly realms because we are united with Christ." Ephesians 1:3 NLT.*

I made up my mind to become the person that the Lord already had called me to be. Walking in my future self. We are made in His image according to His likeness. Each person carries a unique fingerprint, retina scan and dental records– and if that's the case, I was unique. God made me for a special purpose. I had a unique brand identifier and that is what I wanted to begin to articulate.

I started listing the areas that would represent my personal brand. I knew as a company, the brand told a story and had various components which created a successful brand. Could I have similar components that would help articulate my unique personal brand? The answer was Yes. I looked internally at what made me tick as well as what areas made me irritated.

"My brethren, count it all joy when you fall into various trials, knowing that the testing of your faith produces patience. But let patience have its perfect work, that you may be perfect and complete, lacking nothing." James 1:2-4 NKJV

The Lord gave me a new perspective when it came to this verse. The emphasis I had at first with this verse was to rejoice when these trials came. It was my responsibility to change directions. Stop getting mad, frustrated or tempted and instead rejoice and be filled with joy. This was challenging and difficult to comprehend. Through prayer the Lord broadened my understanding of this verse. The trials and temptations were there to reveal something deep down inside that needed to be excavated. Wow, this meant that whatever made me mad or upset, the opposite could carry so much more power. For example, injustice was something that would cause my feathers to ruffle; but acknowledging that I could proactively release justice and be fair created a much more powerful approach. I learned that identifying the opposite of what made my skin crawl was in fact the very thing that produced life.

So, I wrote down and defined my core values. I determined to be very intentional on who I was and my personal brand. My core values also became part of a filtering system. This also empowered me to establish healthy boundaries versus isolating myself with barriers.

Another important learning moment was finding out my style. How did I communicate and what were some things that I cherished? I like working as a team and I enjoy fast-paced environments with clear objectives. I also prefer to be mission oriented with a spirit of generosity. Knowing my communication style was important to become a better communicator with others. How I sounded with a friend, colleague or client became a goal of mine to continue to improve. This was my brand, me, because the Lord in His infinite ability made me unique according to His likeness. It was my job and mission to discover who He called me to be. I read books about leadership, communication and became a student of personality assessments. It became more intriguing to learn about me and the results were remarkable to see how I became a better communicator with those around me. No longer was I stuck in a rut, only attracting and able to get along with the people that were just like me. I became more diversified and created boundaries to help navigate multiple styles of communication.

I started to notice that my core values, the things I

cherished, became more prevalent and I didn't dismiss as many things as I did in the past. I quit abdicating responsibility and took control, which made me more intentional and present. I enjoyed being healthier and being in a healthy place and I wanted to sustain it. In the past my defense mechanisms and barriers isolated me which caused me to retreat, now I created boundaries which help me navigate the different circumstances that arise in life.

"Keep your heart with all diligence, for out of it spring the issues of life." Proverbs 4:23 NKJV

This scripture helped me illustrate this area in my life. Your heart is surrounded by a ribcage. If you let your heart go beyond the rib cage, metaphorically, you open yourself up to heartache and heartbreak. This is the reason for creating healthy boundaries, so you can keep particular situations at bay before they affect you and your heart adversely. Remember, we are to take every thought captive and we are in control of our feelings.

Developing my core values and understanding my style as well as learning the styles of others was an integral part in creating my brand. Plus, this was downright liberating. I could see Me and it made sense. For too long I was in a vicious cycle, living in survival mode, not really cognizant of who I was. Even throughout my years in school I don't recall being taught about Me. The Lord, in His grace brought me along this part of the journey to show me who He intended me to be.

Regarding the components of the brand, I noticed that companies have a mission statement and I could see how my passions could fit here. What I was passionate about was what I loved to talk about the most. It was my heart cord and had the power to resonate with those who felt the same or had similar paths. The more I spoke about my passions, such as seeing people get free from things that were holding them back and having breakthrough moments, the more I saw opportunities materialize.

The final component of creating my personal brand was the community or tribe that I gravitated toward and came across my path. The Lord showed me how this was vital to all of our growth and sustainability.

"From whom the whole body, joined and knit together by what every joint supplies, according to the effective working by which every part does its share, causes growth of the body for the edifying of itself in love." Ephesians 4:16 NKJV

I no longer had to have the Lone Ranger mindset. It was a community effort and something I began to cherish. "Community" when broken down is "commune" – to eat and fellowship. "Unity" is when we are on point or the same page. So I saw a group of people who fellowshipped, ate, and were on the same page with each other. Community became very crucial in my success. As I continued to grow, the people with similar passions and mindsets were attracted to my circle. Also, in the same manner, the people who were not supposed to be in my circle ended up moving on.

"And they continued steadfastly in the apostles' doctrine and fellowship, in the breaking of bread, and in prayers. Then fear came upon every soul, and many wonders and signs were done through the apostles. Now all who believed were together, and had all things in common, and sold their possessions and goods, and divided them among all, as anyone had need.

So continuing daily with one accord in the temple, and breaking bread from house to house, they ate their food with gladness and simplicity of heart, praising God and having favor with all the people. And the Lord added to the church daily those who were being saved." Acts 2:42-47 NLT

Along with developing the brand identifiers for me I was aware in order to keep these changes I needed to create foundational systems:

1 – Be a lifelong learner

"The way of life winds upward for the wise." Proverbs 15:24a NKJV

I read books, listened to speakers, attended workshops. What I found is that I loved learning and could see results. Every area I put through this process was beginning to yield the return that I always desired. I was healthier physically. My walk with the Lord was growing more and more every day. I continued to gain more understanding and overall was so much happier. I woke up and became connected to the life that I prayed for.

"The thief does not come except to steal, and to kill, and to destroy. I have come that they may have life, and that they may have it more abundantly." John 10:10 NKJV

2 – Be coachable

"All Scripture is given by inspiration of God, and is profitable for doctrine, for reproof, for correction, for instruction in righteousness, that the man of God may be complete, thoroughly equipped for every good work." 2 Timothy 3:16 NKJV

As a lifelong learner, I desired to grow with people around me who would be, and were capable of speaking truth into my life. You are the average of the top five people you hang around with the most. I wanted to make sure the people with whom I surrounded myself were going to push me to be who the Lord called me to be. I realized the importance of the support system, not only to speak the truth but also be a source of strength and encouragement.

"I urge you, my brothers and sisters, for the sake of the name of our Lord Jesus Christ, to agree to live in unity with one another and put to rest any division that attempts to tear you apart. Be restored as one united body living in perfect harmony. Form a consistent choreography among yourselves, having a common perspective with shared values." 1 Corinthians 1:10 TPT

3 – Become a better communicator

Let your conversation be always full of grace, seasoned with salt, so that you may know how to answer everyone." Colossians 4:6 NIV

This principle has reaped benefits in every area of my life as a husband, father, friend, minister and business professional. I no longer took for granted the ability to communicate; I was able to develop a desire to learn and grow as a better communicator. Becoming a better communicator, I became a better listener. The discipline to know when to listen or when to listen and respond has been extremely helpful.

"A wise man will hear and increase learning, And a man of understanding will attain wise counsel." Proverbs 1:5 NKJV

I took time to assess all the different modules and information gleaned on the journey. I wrote out what I learned and analyzed the data collected. I did see improvements which was encouraging. I was growing and loved learning. Now I was ready for the next step. How was all of this going to work and fit together?

7 CONVERGENCE

"Three are even better, for a triple-braided cord is not easily broken."
Ecclesiastes 4:12 NLT

I saw myself getting closer to the Lord and who He called me to be. The more I stayed with the process I began to see the correlation with my walk with the Lord and the personal development journey I was on. I was gaining clarity and could see things coming into perfect harmony.

The fragmented ways of life were replaced with a beautiful blend which created an easier flow. The biggest development was when I experienced my passion being blended into the mix. This combination of the different arenas in the spiritual, personal and professional development caused a surge of super charged enthusiasm in me. I stepped into the person God created me to be, walking out what He created me to do and possessed clarity to communicate the vision laid out before me. This was convergence.

Convergence is the act of moving toward union or uniformity. God was taking my life as a minister and a professional through a period of convergence. The place where everything collided. This was the exact place where God wanted me to be. All the pieces began to fall into place.

Looking back, it was difficult at first to have such a passion for ministry, only to discover an affinity for the marketplace. Where did I fit? I desired to find my place.

From the age of sixteen, I knew that preaching was a huge aspect of my calling. I pursued the ministry and went directly into Bible college. On one side I wanted to speak globally to evangelize and the other part of me had a strong desire to see local communities impacted. I worked in the children's and youth ministries with the students along with developing programs and writing curriculum. I served as an associate pastor along with traveling to speak at other churches. As time passed I worked in various parts of the ministry including missions, community outreach and much more, learning the ins and outs of the church.

My passion was being fueled by serving in the ministry, and years after college I launched a church where all of my skills were needed to recruit volunteers, cast the vision, hire music staff and run the day-to-day operations for the ministry. At the time I could only see the current moment, usually feeling as if the moment was running me and not me running the moment.

I found myself often praying, asking God for

direction and next steps. This time was a huge training season in my life. I loved ministering and helping others while my internal development and communication skills were being defined and sharpened behind the scenes.

In between fulltime ministry and raising money to fund the ministry calling I found myself getting plugged into the corporate world. What a shift from non-profit to profit. The structure was appealing and I found my competitive side kick in gear when I had a product or service to sell.

Side note: Knowing where you are and where you came from is essential to pick out the clues to discovering the calling of God on your life.

I remember working in my early teens to make extra money and even paid cash for my first car at the age of sixteen. I was accustomed to working and earning income. I even found my entrepreneurial side by teaching private swimming lessons. This too surfaced as an internal desire. I knew I would need money to fund the ministry and fulfill what God called me to accomplish. Plus, if He gave me the vision, then He would give me the provision. It was around then that I started to develop an acumen for the business world. Strategies, market share, profitability, communication and leadership were all appealing to me. The innovation and creativity that the marketplace possessed was truly inspiring.

The professional arena was exciting and for the most part enjoyable. However, the vacillating thoughts of being a full-time minister or full-time professional always seemed to nag at my conscience. I didn't have complete understanding why God would give me such a passion for helping people and a new found love for the marketplace. In my work-life experience I developed skill sets, disciplines and an affinity for business. I enjoyed the numbers, metrics, and strategic planning. I loved the pursuit of the project and overcoming obstacles, challenges and producing a winning solution.

How was this supposed to happen? I could definitely relate to the ministry and had a large interest for the marketplace.

The great thing were the principles throughout the Bible had an application in personal life and in business; and the Lord gave me eyes to see how they could become harmoniously aligned. I began to create programs which incorporated the spiritual, personal and professional development through the leading of the Holy Spirit. As I created, He began opening up avenues that I could see His hand working in every aspect from leadership, communication, destiny and systems. It was super intense and exciting to be able to follow the guiding of His hand and see the creation of the program.

"Being confident of this very thing, that He who has begun a good work in you will complete it until the day of Jesus Christ." Philippians 1:6 NKJV

In the developmental stages of these programs I was aware of how much separation there is when it comes to different areas in our life. While I am a firm believer in compartmentalization, I see the connection side being equally as important. Taking our physical makeup as an example, the hand is an important part of the body; however, the hand cannot function without being attached to the arm. Connection was important to me and I created a model to represent the interdependence of how everything working together affects the whole.

"Even so the body is not made up of one part but of many. Now if the foot should say, 'Because I am not a hand, I do not belong to the body,' it would not for that reason stop being part of the body. And if the ear should say, 'Because I am not an eye, I do not belong to the body,'' it would not for that reason stop being part of the body.' 1 Corinthians 12:14-16 NIV

I learned He will complete the work inside of us if we surrender. Hindsight is 20/20, so they say; however, I can see His handiwork throughout my life to bring me right where I need to be. The things that you and I have been through up to this point has made us to be the person who we are now. In God's kingdom, operating system and environment, there is nothing wasted. He uses every minute detail and every major event to form and fashion us to be prepared to fulfill what He has given to us.

"For this is the love of God, that we keep His commandments. And His commandments are not burdensome." 1 John 5:3 NKJV

I pressed into the Lord and did what I felt He asked me to do. There were times in this process that I didn't know if I was going to make it, and other times that I felt on top of the world. It was a time to listen and keep the faith that the dreams I had when I was younger would come to pass. I could look back and see the training ground in the ministry and marketplace coming together. I could see that my presentation skills developed in the pulpit, my creativity, and an innovative approach sharpened through the professional journey. The people I came across and relationships built had a massive impact on my development. The ability to preach behind the pulpit gave me confidence to step out on the stage. God gave me eyes of understanding to translate the principles in His word into marketplace language to reach a new audience.

While I was going through the internal process from my model, the Lord also led me to discover further more how the personal, professional and spiritual application to this model were all intertwined. The more I looked I could see many applications to this process which were exhilarating. Moving toward my calling, I was continually thanking God for being omniscient and opening my eyes to see new revelations.

What I experienced personally and professionally through creating these programs would now be able to be shared with others by teaching and mentoring.

In this season I found my platform to share my signature message. Everything converged, I was exactly where the Lord wanted me to be and I was at peace to know everything that I went through, the good the bad and the indifferent. I was the man who God created me to be. I know whose I am, who I am and what I am here for.

In sharing my message I saw wonderful results. I

saw lives touched on many levels and was encouraged by the testimonies to hear how my clients experienced an impact in their lives spiritually, personally and professionally. The message resonated and released such a powerful dynamic, touching lives in many facets. After speaking to groups, I would learn about the various areas where the message resonated with these groups of professionals, from the spiritual, personal and professional arenas. My heart was full of joy. It was surreal to be in a place where God called you to be and have the liberty and freedom to function at that level.

I continued to create programs to ultimately see the restoration of families, neighborhoods, communities and cities. I knew the marketplace had truly gifted people with the creativity and innovation to make a difference; and teaching these principles to people who are involved in the marketplace would impact them and their families.

This platform was, and still is, marketplace ministry. All of my skills, gifts, talents were developed for this. My circumstances and experiences all worked out by the Lord to equip me for such a time as this. My audience expanded from the four walls of the church building to the four corners of the globe. God brought me to a higher place than I could see in the beginning. He brought me up and out of some places where visibility was bleak. It was God who called me and He is faithful to bring it to pass. My eyes now open to this new place in the Lord. Now was the time to go full force to accomplish the task.

8 MY MESSAGE

"For your very lives are our "letters of recommendation," permanently engraved on our hearts, recognized and read by everybody. As a result of our ministry, you are living letters written by Christ, not with ink but by the Spirit of the living God—not carved onto stone tablets but on the tablets of tender hearts." 2 Corinthians 3:2-3 TPT

When I began to see how all of these seasons of my life came together inspired me to create my message—not just any message, but my signature message. It couldn't be any ordinary message; it had to have certain criteria that would resonate above all other messages. I knew my platform and laid out my programs; now I needed a vehicle to deliver my message.

I mapped out a plan. In the middle of the piece of paper I added more to the envelope illustration. I extended the vertical line from the envelope to the bottom of the page. This began to make sense and became clearer as I continued. The drawing was a cross with God's calling for my life in the envelope intersecting with the horizontal plane where I was called to fulfill it. The center of the cross represented the very core of my being, when everything is properly aligned to God's will and I'm walking in His purpose for my life.

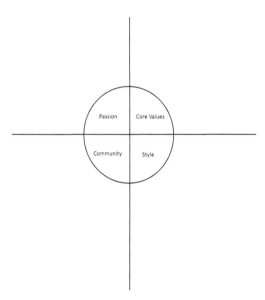

I drew a circle around the center of the cross and in one section wrote *Core Values*, in the other section I scribbled *Passion*, in the third quadrant I wrote *Style,* and in the fourth area I wrote *Community*. I saw this part of the illustration look more like a beacon that was broadcasting a sound. I drew sound waves that came from the center and it was exciting to see that my signature message evolved from the core of whose I was and who I was and what I was put on this earth to accomplish. The saying we often hear is "Just speak from the heart." This was it – the message stemmed from the center of the cross.

"Then He said to them all, 'If anyone desires to come after Me, let him deny himself, and take up his cross daily, and follow Me.'" Luke 9:23 NKJV

I poured out my heart. My passion flowed easily on paper writing about serving God, advancing His kingdom through helping others identify their calling, and helping them create plans so they could see their calling fulfilled. It was natural to write about how to help others break out of cycles to see results. I also included my style in how I enjoy operating. Team and mission oriented, fast paced with several things working at once. This was my working

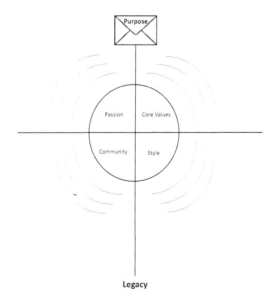

environment where I was the most effective. My core values in my message expressed who I was and the beliefs which were important to me, such as truth, fair scales and justice. The passion which burns inside of me mixed with my core values and style was a powerful combination.

What about my target audience? Whom do I serve, and was my passion directed to the correct audience? Needing to map out the audience, I wrote the goals, objectives and overall vision of what I wanted to accomplish.

"Write the vision and make it plain on tablets, that he may run who reads it. For the vision is yet for an appointed time; but at the end it will speak, and it will not lie. Though it tarries, wait for it; because it will surely come, it will not tarry." Habakkuk 2:2-3 NKJV

Creating the template for my message helped speed up the process. Structure wasn't always the easiest area for me to develop; however, when I learned to become more disciplined, then structure was essential for me. I could still navigate the unstructured and sporadic parts of life but I thrived better in a structured format. I learned I could be more flexible with more structure.

What did I want my audience to walk away with? What were the steps in the process that would lead them to reach this destination? This was the next step in developing my message. I needed to write out clear, attainable objectives; for example, effectively communicating the process on how someone gets clarity on their heavenly assignment. Or steps to strategically align their current model to achieve maximum results. Once I got the objectives laid out in the order that made sense, I went back to expand on each of the points for my message. This was the substance of the message. It needed to have some antidotes that would result in true life changes. I had to dive deeper into these sections' subject matter and pull from other sources to articulate my points. The result of this part of the exercise was I learned more about me. I am so grateful to the Lord because it doesn't matter what we are doing; His hands are working in and through us continuously. Writing out my message gave me solid footing to stand on. My vision was clear and the objectives were substantial to deliver the right results, which brought me to the next section. What were the goals for my message? Along with the vision I drew out the next steps and path to get my audience from start to finish.

Another great part of telling my story was walking in freedom of who the Lord called me to be. Plus, I have seen that the story is ongoing and my passion to help people discover who God has called them to be expands as I continue to press into the Lord.

We are moving from faith to faith and glory to glory. The skills become more defined in the situations we overcome and victories we win continue to be added to our stories.

My experiences were embraced at a much deeper level. I learned to embrace the lessons and story lines throughout my life which in turn would benefit others.

We are the message. Taking all of my life situations, circumstances, victories and battles have made me who I am today. The gold nugget in this process is that every person has a story and that story needs to be articulated in strategic way to help others along the way.

My overall mission is to help people identify and fulfill their God-given calling. It was more than just helping identify, it was to identify and put together a plan to fulfill. What would that entail and how could I take this message to the world and help people? So I began to write more. I wrote speeches, sermons, blogs and letters. I discovered that if I stayed with the structures and disciplines that I learned throughout the journey the same principles applied to every area. I developed more structure. The revelation of my personal message also opened up; and as I looked back at previous writings, there were similar themes:

- I am advancing the Kingdom of God by

  _____

- Helping people fulfill their God-Given calling and assignment
- Bridging the gap between your business and God's business
- Combining faith and practicality
- Transforming lives through personal and professional development
- Initiate the reflection of change
- Advance God's Kingdom through the marketplace
- Equipping people to do the work of ministry

My message became a part of me, it was me. My

core values as well as style were fueled by my passion. My signature message of who I was and what the Lord has called me to accomplish. I shared parts of my struggles and victories, the lessons I learned along the way to encourage those who might be taking similar paths. I also created a plan to share my story with objectives to inspire and equip others to take the step of faith to believe God for the purpose of their lives. As I began to share my personal story I saw amazing doors which opened me up to more opportunities. People with whom I had the privilege to share my story would in turn have the courage to share their own. It became easier to help people find their story. The message inside of me was coming alive. It was fascinating to watch it evolve. I could see growth in me and see growth in others.

"All things work together for good, for those who love God; to those who are called according to His purpose." Romans 8:28 NKJV

My message didn't put me into a box—it actually had the opposite effect. It opened up countless possibilities and doors that I hadn't recognized before. This stage of the journey was fun to wake up to every morning. Even in the rough patches, which we all encounter, I found new strength to rise up, press through. This was my life, my passion and I grew deeper in my relationship with the Lord. This message connected me to the people whom the Lord wanted me to serve and again opened my eyes to additional audiences. It was full of life, encouragement and hope. It was a message people could relate to and it resonated deep within their hearts. It was the message that explained my unique brand. I knew we all have a message to be shared. The combination of our situations, circumstances, gifts and skill sets along with the bumps, bruises, hurts and pains. These all were the culmination of all of who I am today and who we all are. This message brought people liberty and helped them find freedom. It was exciting to learn to be me. My true authentic self, the person that God created me to be. I got rid of fear, shame and guilt knowing that this was about being me, battle tested and strengthened to help others.

"There is therefore now no condemnation to those who are in Christ Jesus, who do not walk according to the flesh, but according to the Spirit." Romans 8:1 NKJV

This scripture rang louder and louder. God took all of me and through the power of Christ Jesus brought me to a victorious place in Him.

"Now thanks be to God who always leads us in triumph in Christ, and through us diffuses the fragrance of His knowledge in every place." 2 Corinthians 2:14 NKJV

I found great comfort in being me and sharing my story. It was healing and enlightening not just personally but to those I was around. No more trying to be perfect and putting on a show so people would accept me. I came to a place where in my message I knew that I was loved, accepted and approved of by God. Walking in that truth and sharing my message is truly impactful and life-changing.

God has a wonderful plan for you and as you move into Part Two I pray you will find the keys to unlock all that the Lord has in store for you. God is no respecter of persons and what He does for one He will do for you. You have a story to share and will find the abundant life He has for you as you walk out your calling. Enjoy the journey and I will see you in Part Two.

Brian

PART TWO

9 WHERE DO I START?

How many times in life are you asked, "Where are you?" If we really dive into the question, isn't the context more specifically, "Where are you *in life at any given moment?*" That is the big ticket question and it is often times difficult to conceptualize. In this chapter I want to bring you to a heightened awareness of where you are at. It's like walking into a large theme park and your first objective is to find a map of where you are so you can make the most out of your experience.

Let's take a good look at where we are today–in work, family, finances, and so on. This is the first step that brings a conscious awareness of the various areas that we experience in life. While this is not a line by line detailed list about everything, it does serve as a tool to compartmentalize areas so we can effectively improve the specific while improving as a whole.

As we draw closer to God and what we are called to do, God at the same time is working in us and through us. So the appropriate posture is to keep a healthy balance of knowing we are being developed and we're fulfilling our calling. The complexity is that we have many things to attend to; however, the Lord is gracious to give us the roadmap to accomplish all that He has put into our hearts to accomplish.

"But he who looks into the perfect law of liberty and continues in it, and is not a forgetful hearer but a doer of the work, this one will be blessed in what he does." James 1:25 NKJV

This is an area where I often got stuck. I was trying to perform to get the assignment of the Lord accomplished. While fixed on the mission, I still was aware that the Lord wanted my heart. However, this was only a portion of what the Lord desired. He gave us a spirit that I will reference as your heart, and a mind in which I separate the intellectual and emotional aspects and body to honor him. As I spent time with the Lord I noticed areas in my life where I lacked good stewardship, and once I started working on these areas, my purpose seemed to get clearer as well. There is a definite correlation between your calling and you personally. As we focus on the areas of stewardship you will discover that there are similar principles which also relate to the God-given calling.

"And now, Israel, what does the Lord your God require of you, but to fear the Lord your God, to walk in all His ways and to love Him, to serve the Lord your God with all your heart and with all your soul, and to keep the commandments of the Lord and His statutes which I command you today for your good?" Deuteronomy 10:12-13 NKJV

I am typically asked after a presentation if I work with individuals and if I could help them with their business. The answer is Yes, and I schedule a time with them to see what results they are looking to receive. In a particular situation, I was approached by a person who wanted help in her business. She needed to increase her productivity to increase her income. On our initial meeting, as I do for most every client, I got a list of goals and answers to a questionnaire that I sent out prior to our meeting. When we sat down to meet I quickly discovered that money was not the problem (and typically it isn't the answer). So, I drew out the personal battery pack model (covered in Chapter Three) and went over each area, and asked my client to score herself on how she perceived each battery, or area in her life. Once we finished the scoring I quickly added up the scores and divided by eight to get the average. Interestingly, the score was in the low 40s. I asked if this was accurate and she sadly agreed. From that moment, the direction of increasing productivity shifted to creating action items to increase the overall life score. It looked as if we were deviating from the original plan, but I assured her that if she would work on increasing this score, then the other areas of concern would improve as well. We took the three lowest areas (in her case it was physical, business and marriage/family), and developed a simple action plan with the three. After a few short weeks, I got a call from my client that her productivity is increasing at her job. During our next session she was excited to share and began telling me that doing the action items we listed helped boost her confidence and improved her self-esteem. She wanted to re-score herself and watched the average move to the mid-sixties. She explained that this exercise helped her become more focused and intentional in her life, which also led to more intentionality in her business. The overall process continued to get improved results from both the personal and professional arenas. This is one of many stories using the Battery Pack Life Score Exercise and as we dive into eight areas you will begin to assess where you are and what activities are going to improve in these areas.

No more excuses. This is not a quick band-aid approach or the time to disassociate. This is the time to see transformation and become who God called you to be. Too often we try to fix the top layer or just the symptoms when actually it would be more beneficial to look at the cause to see true change. Our root systems determine our fruit systems and the Bible says that we are to bear fruit.

"By this My Father is glorified, that you bear much fruit; so you will be My disciples." John 15:8 NKJV

This exercise is designed to map out eight domains or areas in our lives:

Spiritual. Love the Lord with all of your heart. God created us first and foremost to have a relationship with Him. As a loving heavenly father, He gave us a free will and access to Him at anytime and anywhere. Our relationship with the Father is the very cornerstone of our faith and causes all the surrounding areas to work.

"My own sheep will hear my voice and I know each one, and they will follow me. I give to them the gift of eternal life and they will never be lost and no one has the power to snatch them out of my hands." John 10:27-28 NKJV

Intellectual. The intellectual side of us is the capacity to reason and comprehend. It is where the human will sits and choices are made. Are we growing, studying and reading to improve? Are we coachable and committed to be a life-long learner? It is good to gain knowledge and understanding that we can steward our thoughts.

"Commit your works to the Lord, And your thoughts will be established." Proverbs 16:3 NKJV

Emotional. The emotional aspect of life is where we feel and exercise our five senses. We all have feelings and the extremes are not only noticeable but unhealthy. The ones who choose not to feel while others are completely driven by emotions.

"Blessed be the God and Father of our Lord Jesus Christ, the Father of mercies and God of all comfort, who comforts us in all our tribulation, that we may be able to comfort those who are in any trouble, with the comfort with which we ourselves are comforted by God." 2 Corinthians 1:3-4 NKJV

Physical. The physical aspect is comprised of our

overall health in a physical state. I am a big believer that the Lord wants us to be healthy in all areas including physical. Are we eating healthy? What about getting a good night's sleep or even exercising? Our bodies belong to the Lord and it is good for us to be healthy to accomplish all that He has for us.

"At the end of the ten days they looked healthier and better nourished than any of the young men who ate the royal food. So the guard took away their choice food and the wine they were to drink and gave them vegetables instead." Daniel 1:15-16 NIV

Marriage/Family. How do we perceive our closest relationships? This is not taking on a surface level approach but asking for the feedback, whether from your biological family or a group that you consider family. This area is important because God has established family units for our protection and blessing.

"But as for me and my house, we will serve the Lord." Joshua 24:15 NKJV

Financial/Lifestyle. This identifies two primary areas that we strive and work for, your freedom of time and your financial independence. Too often we experience one or the other or in some cases we don't possess either.

- Do you have a financial plan, budget or goals?
- What is your ultimate net worth number?

- Are you able to go where you want, when you want for as long as you want?
- What is your life purpose and what does that look like?

"Glorify God with all your wealth, honoring him with your very best, with every increase that comes to you. Then every dimension of your life will overflow with blessings from an uncontainable source of inner joy!" Proverbs 3:8-10 TPT

Business. There are many metrics with a business we can and should measure to calculate growth and overall health of the organization. This category should be scored on a level of satisfaction and fulfillment. Are you in survival mode, not enough or abundance? How would you categorize what you are doing to earn a living currently? Is it a job, career or your calling?

"And whatever you do, do it heartily, as to the Lord and not to men." Colossians 3:23 NKJV

Social. This is where you rate how well you're connected to your community. What does your inner circle look like? How would you rate your relationship to your friends, colleagues and acquaintances?

"How good and pleasant it is when God's people live together in unity!" Psalm 133:1 NIV

The more connected we are to these areas, the more success we will see. It is easy for us to dismiss one area over the other or completely turn away from an area where we don't see the value.

Working for several months with another client and hitting roadblock after roadblock, the sessions became more of an excuse-dump versus a next step action plan. I would come in with a set agenda and ask if the previous steps that we set up were accomplished, and my client's answer was, "I'm just too busy and I don't have time." This went on for the next couple of meetings with me reconfiguring plans to accomplish the goals only to no avail. On the next meeting my client broke the silence and disclosed that his personal life was in shambles and it was almost unbearable. I immediately understood the disconnect. He was not able to go further until he stopped the energy drain. I explained the independent and interdependent model of the battery pack and we set temporary goals to get back on track. His countenance changed and instantly he felt the energy shift because he had a plan that was in place.

Some things just don't get better over time. We are responsible for all areas and the more intentional we become in creating an overall healthy score then we become proactive and not reactive. So, how do you measure the intangibles in life? Your perception is your reality; therefore if you score yourself based on how you perceive any given area, then you can establish a metric system to use for growth.

This tool is designed for you to assess where you are currently as well as help you discover what you need to do in order to progress and how to measure the results.

This Battery Pack gives you a total average and specific averages in order to be able to become more strategic in bringing up your score in one area or overall score on life. This model will compartmentalize the eight areas to identify individual parts as well as show the interdependence in how they are all working together. The scoring system is on a 0-90 point system:

- 90 points for an A
- 80-89 points for a B
- 70-79 points for a C
- 60-69 points for a D
- 0-59 points is not passing

Now it's time to take the assessment. In each area score yourself based on your perception of how you are doing. For example, you might score yourself an 85 in the spiritual area and a 70 in the physical area. Once you have scored yourself in all eight areas add all the numbers up and divide by 8. This will give you the overall average of where you are. Make a note of each one of the battery cells and how you scored yourself. Plus, look at the overall score of the exercise. You can see how each cell contributes to the whole.

Finding your calling and accomplishing all the Lord had laid on your heart is connected in who we are and what we do. By taking action in each area, I am convinced you will find yourself moving in the direction that God has for you.

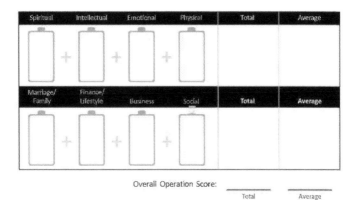

Spiritual	Intellectual	Emotional	Physical	Total	Average
Marriage/ Family	Finance/ Lifestyle	Business	Social	Total	Average

Overall Operation Score: _____ _____

                                   Total   Average

10 TAKE ACTION

After you score yourself with the battery pack and find the three lowest scores, write each one down on a piece of paper. Underneath each one I want you to write actionable items for each of the three that you will commit to doing to improve your score. The key in accomplishing these items is as simple as applying a 1% rule. The 1% rule is the smallest basic item done over a long period of time will produce results.

This is the time to make true progress. Time to take action. It is one thing to dream about a task or think about something you would like to see or get the results you want; it is another thing to pick up the slack and start taking action.

I have seen this happen with numerous clients. Occasionally we're caught up in a situation that seems to be insurmountable; when in reality stepping back helps us get a clearer picture of what is going on. I had a gentleman ask me to help with his business. As I worked with him it became apparent that the problem was not at all what was discussed in the beginning. So, I asked my client to write down a detailed report of his daily schedule for Monday through Friday and email it to me before the next meeting.

During our next meeting I recommended adjusting the day to day activities and gave him small incremental tasks for each day. In the first month he saw an increase in his numbers and by the end of ninety days he saw a significant jump in productivity. I received a call from him a few years later thanking me and he informed me that he sold his company for a great profit and is moving into other ventures. The small things may look irrelevant and miniscule but when you do them consistently you will find amazing results.

"Truly I tell you, if you have faith as small as a mustard seed, you can say to this mountain, 'Move from here to there,' and it will move. Nothing will be impossible for you." Matthew 17:20 NKJV

Now you should have selected three areas to improve, plus one to three action items for each area that you can work on. Determine the best time to accomplish these activities: morning, during the day or evening. Once you have decided where they fit, choose if the activity is something you can do throughout the day, which is what I call activity blocking, or is this an activity that you need to have a set time for such as reading, studying or devotion.

My example of activity blocking is this. Let's say you create a business goal to make fifteen phone calls a day. The night before you type an email to yourself with the fifteen names, phone numbers and notes for the call. In the subject line you put Daily Call Log with tomorrow's date. Hit send. When you wake up in the morning you have in your inbox an email waiting for you. This is your activity and throughout your busy day you can open your email at any free time you get and work your way through the call list. At the end of the day you have made fifteen calls and have an email trail for your records. The end of the year if you want to verify your records then you can type in the search bar of your email account Daily Call Log and the list of emails you sent to yourself will populate.

This exercise is encouraging to me because I know that if I focus on any one area of my life, create a small task and do it, then I see results. Not only do I see the results in this individual area, it also increases my overall average that translates improvement and a happier attitude.

Now, let's take a life goal that you have. What does it look like? Where would you like to be in the next 60-90 days? That first image is critical because it is the pattern or visual aid that we will use to get us to achieve the goal at hand. No different than the goal line in football–if you know where you are headed, it's a lot easier to get there.

Write down your goal. After writing it down I want you to break this down into small actionable items that you can accomplish on a day-to-day basis. Don't get into a rush with writing down a multitude of items down. This is the time to be more thorough with your list.

Basically, you are creating the pathway. When you look at these items, try to determine what needs to happen, before and after, that will keep you on track. For example, if you want to get into shape, you would know that you need to find a gym or a place to work out. Then you would need to find a workout program and schedule that time. The items before your actual activity are on your path as well, meaning that if you scheduled your workout time for 6:00 AM every morning, then getting your workout clothes ready the night before and placing them where you get dressed will aid in creating a path of least resistance. This will help you stay consistent and not allow your brain to take over with excuses. It is very similar to the people who like to eat healthy will take time to meal prep beforehand. After your workout is complete, what steps are needed to get you back into starting your day? Do you drink a protein shake? Have the ingredients readily available to keep you in the flow. When you are creating your path you are actually taking the thinking out of the equation by being prepared beforehand; and then when the time comes to take action it is a lot easier.

Another example of this is when you are planning on going on vacation. We make the necessary arrangements to prepare so we can enjoy our trip–writing down our list of items to pack, checking the gas in the car, making sure we have our plane tickets, and checking the alarm clock several times so we don't oversleep. We also spend the day or night before our trip to pack and set everything up, so when it is time to leave we can jump into the car and go on our way.

These same principles can be applied to goal setting. You need to become a fantastic planner. Think of things you might need before and after the activity. Plan those things ahead of time. As you go through these processes you can always make changes or modifications to make your path better. The longer you do this you begin to find a rhythm in your process and it becomes natural.

Once you get into the rhythm and you feel settled then you begin to gain momentum. Gaining momentum allows you to add other areas or goals to the mix and do the same thing–getting a pathway mapped out and then being consistent doing that to gain momentum in other areas.

Your Thought Life and Conscious Awareness

If you are not cognizant about where you are and what you are doing, it will not only be difficult but merely impossible to change. It is essential to be present and not become distracted and start to drift. You are in control of your thoughts and it will benefit you to become more conscientious as you journey through the process.

In a workshop I was presenting, person in the audience came up to me and said, "Wow, you really made me think." Good. That's what is supposed to happen. It is easy to put our minds on autopilot, and it takes work to be intentional and present; however, the result in being present far outweighs the other. Change comes from our mind, first and foremost. If you don't change the way you think, it is going to be impossible to change the way you act and behave.

Three areas for heightening your awareness:

1. In order to change our thoughts, we need to be aware of our environment and have a correct or healthy world-view. This occurs when you can see your surroundings from God's perspective and not your own. What is going on around you? If you could

describe the environment where you are the most productive, what would it look like?

"The kingdom of God is not eating and drinking, but righteousness and
peace and joy in the Holy Spirit." Romans 14:17 NKJV

If you look at this verse you can see that the operating environment of God's kingdom
is righteousness, which is order, peace and joy. I function best and get more accomplished when my environment is peaceful, orderly and happy. A chaotic and cluttered environment only leads to frustration and inefficiency. An environment full of fear, anxiety and stress leads to confusion.

2. Check your internal dialogue. What are the things you say to yourself? Sometimes it is better just to be still and quiet your mind so you can begin to discern what is happening on the inside.

"Be still and know that I am God." Psalm 46:10 NKJV
"In quietness and confidence shall be your strength." Isaiah 30:15 NKJV

Being still and quiet without any external noises can be challenging to find. I often recommend
to my clients to find a quiet place away from their phones, emails, computers and other noises.

Take a pen and a notebook and practice sitting there for five or more minutes in complete silence. As things surface in your brain, jot them down in your notebook and continue to sit until your time is up. This exercise has really been helpful for me personally to be able to reset and clear my head. The focus I receive afterwards always increases and I am more effective. If you can be comfortable in silence then you can find your way through the noise.

3. Check your external stimuli. Who and what are you allowing to enter into your thoughts? The outside noise, influences and voices have an impact whether we acknowledge them or not. Words are a creative force and we need to be more aware of what we allow to enter in. It helps to set activities to feed your mind with positive, life-giving thoughts.

    "And now, dear brothers and sisters, one final thing. Fix your thoughts on what is true, and honorable, and right, and pure, and lovely, and admirable. Think about things that are excellent and worthy of praise." Philippians 4:8 NLT

    The more you feed yourself with positive information the better you become. This builds you up internally and creates a strength that will be necessary moving you through the various seasons of life. Be more intentional to listen to books, podcasts and educate yourself throughout your week. Read a great book and have positive quotes around you for reminders.

Your Feelings

Developing a good posture on your feelings will cause strength to rise in you. We can either let our feelings control us, which makes us more reactive, or we can be proactive regarding our feelings. This scripture gives us many examples about emotions and feelings. Jesus even says that our joy should be made full.

"But the Holy Spirit produces this kind of fruit in our lives: love, joy, peace, patience, kindness, goodness, faithfulness, gentleness, and self-control. There is no law against these things!" Galatians 5:22-23 NLT

So, how can we become more in control of our feelings? Happiness first and success will follow. You can choose to be happy. It is your choice and there are key things to maintain a posture of happiness. Here are five actions to heighten your emotional state for happiness and peace:

1. Smile. It takes less effort to smile and it is contagious.
2. Say something positive and look for the good.
3. Compliment someone.
4. Be thankful.
5. Walk in a continual state of forgiveness.

You have mapped out your path for the areas you want to see improvement and you have your thoughts and feelings in check. Continue to seek the Lord and His counsel as you walk out this journey. No one is perfect, and improving should always be in the forefront of our minds. As you continue to seek the Lord, allow Him to guide and direct your steps.

11 THE POWER OF THE PROCESS

You now should have a list of the areas you want to see improve as well as the activities for each area. Knowing what to do is one step in the right direction. Now, we are going to outline the process so we can see the activity come to fruition. The eight phases of transformation model outlined in this book was created to help you identify where you are in the transformation process. This helps to keep you motivated and gives you the next steps to move forward. It is counterproductive to get into any situation and be left in the dark, not knowing where to go and wonder if what you are doing is actually working. Leaving your success up to chance is not a viable option. To continue to do things only to find out that you were doing the wrong things is a horrible place to be.

As we journey through these eight phases you will begin to identify which phase you are in and have the tools to get you to the next level. Knowing where you are in the midst of the process will keep you on the right track, give you the hope you need to press into the process and a place where your mind can go to when it is requires the most focus.

Let's take a good look at each phase to determine

the activities necessary to make progress.

Phase 1 - KIA affect

"The little foxes that spoil the vines." Song of Solomon 2:15 NKJV

The KIA affect, otherwise known as the Know-It-All affect, happens more often than we would like to admit. Let me give you an example. When we go into a situation or circumstance, our brains are looking for the solution to survive and takes us back to what we know or the frame of reference from a past situation or circumstance that was similar.

Wow, this looks easy enough, this is a no-brainer, or I've heard this before. But what happens when we get into this know-it-all mindset is we block out any possibility for growth beyond what we have already experienced in the past. We are not open to broadening our understanding.

If we go back to the parable of the sower in Chapter four, imagine taking the seed for yourself. The seed represents knowledge. What did you do with the seed? You spread the seeds on top of the soil, correct? Yes. The soil represents the mind. If the knowledge only stays on the outskirts of the mind or the seed only stays on top of the soil then what happens? It gets stolen. The birds will eat it or the wind will blow the seeds away.

The lesson here is that you always want to be aware when you are able to receive the knowledge being given, and not reject it because your brain has already shown you a past situation. Or to rephrase the statement, "I already know this."

Knowledge or information needs to go through a process the same as the seed. Remember, that seed contains power of transformation. However, if the seed is not planted correctly, then the seed will go to waste and the ground will never benefit.

The book of Proverbs continuously reminds us to embrace and get wisdom. So, in the first phase of Know it all – the scripture says this area is where the seed falls by the wayside; hard soil is where the enemy steals the seed. *"Humble yourself in the sight of the Lord and He will lift you up." James 4:10 NKJV*. Humility and yielding to become a life-long learner is key. Having the desire to gain more knowledge, wisdom and open yourself up to new perspectives gives you the ability to access Phase 2.

We can always learn in and through every situation. Be open to learning. *"And Jesus increased in wisdom and stature, and in favor with God and men." Luke 2:52 NKJV*

Phase 2 - Idea Zone

Idea Zone is the second phase that I want us to look at. This is the first layer the seed has to go through.

Have you ever been in a place that you had that ah-ha moment? How did you leave that meeting or place? You probably left excited and had a feeling finally something was going to work out in your favor. Why do you think you were excited? It was because you had insight to the knowledge or information which could get you to achieve what you always wanted.

What happens in this level is the mind receives the seed and begins to come up with other possibilities, which makes the brain go to work on solutions and resolutions to current problems. It actually releases endorphins in your mind which makes you feel good. You are familiar with brainstorming, correct? Well, in brainstorming sessions we typically feel rejuvenated and excited because our brains are creatively working.

This is only the beginning because it is the second layer of soil. When you plant the seed in this layer, it has rocks–and if the rocks are not taken out, the seed will sprout without taking root and wither as soon as the sun comes up. Take for example the brainstorming meeting. You and your group came up with these awesome ideas and you all were going to be rich. Several weeks go by and you can barely remember what you learned, let alone where the notes ended up. Who implemented these ideas? Who put time stamps on them and is effectively executing them on a consistent basis? Not many, if any. If you want the seed to take root and grow up you will need to move the seed beyond the rocky soil.

How does this work in everyday life? Picture the rocks as obstacles, hurdles and weaknesses. For instance, we have a great idea. Have we identified our strengths? What about the weaknesses? Plus, do we foresee any obstacles that might come up, and if so, what is the protocol to remedy these? Did we put any time stamps and mile-markers to get this up and running? Who are the key people and what are their roles, responsibilities and expectations? Do we have the right people? Do we have the right tools and resources?

Your activity for this phase is to remove the rocks

in the soil so you can plant the seed properly. Remember, the scripture says the flower immediately springs up and when the sun rises, the flower is scorched because it doesn't have a root system. We have seen and experienced too many times the exciting moment that seemed to be life-changing, only to see it walk away. The feeling of excitement left as quick as it came in. The rocks needed to be removed are idleness and lack of action. To go through this phase you will need to arm your mind with the strategy to implement and execute.

Remembering the account of Joseph interpreting the dream for Pharaoh also comes with a strategy to implement. Read the account of Joseph in Genesis 41: 22-40

"Joseph's suggestions were well received by Pharaoh and his officials." Genesis 41:37 NIV

Phase 3 - Noise Zone

The next layer is the Noise Zone. You've taken the information and mapped out your plan and suddenly you are hearing noises from all around. One because you have just emerged from your long brainstorming session have now entered back into reality.

You are super excited about this idea and piece of knowledge you rush to the phone and you proceed to tell someone that you're going to make it big.

Silence ...pierces through the phone. Something has changed drastically from when they answered. You ask what's wrong? Are you still there? They reply, "Yes, that will never work." Your heart sinks simultaneously as your stomach goes to your throat. You have just experienced part of the Noise Zone.

You tell yourself that this doesn't matter and you keep going but not long after a voice in your head begins to question whether or not this is going to work. The voice inside your head also will remind you of other cares and concerns that will derail your progress.

If you know this going into this area then you can create the mental fortitude to stand your ground and keep believing.

It happens often when people start a diet. They take the new piece of knowledge that they received and begin to talk to their friends, family and co-workers. What ends up happening is that someone they knew tried it and it didn't work.

Remember, it's the seed or knowledge that we plant. If you take the seed and you plant it in soil that has weeds then the weeds will choke out the seed and the seed will not last.

The scripture states this phase is filled with outside cares and concerns aimed to choke out the seed and prevent growth.

Activity in this phase requires you to create healthy boundaries. The two primary boundaries are your heart and your mind.

We are told in scripture to guard our heart and mind. It is time to build your boundary around your heart. This means that your heart is able to go to a certain point and people, situations and circumstances are only allowed to come to a certain point as well.

Look at the rib cage for an illustration. Your rib cage surrounds your heart and if your heart exceeds the boundary it is susceptible to heart-ache or heart-break. The rib cage also serves as a boundary that doesn't allow things to get to close. This gives you the ability to keep things at a healthy distance and only allow what you deem necessary to pass through.

The other boundary is from your mind and that is your thoughts. Take captive every thought and make it come into the obedience of Christ Jesus. This area I found very liberating once I figured out the how-to of this verse.

"We demolish arguments and every pretension that sets itself up against the knowledge of God, and we take captive every thought to make it obedient to Christ." 2 Corinthians 10:5 NIV

The skill set to slow yourself down in the midst of the fast paced society we live in today will be imperative to learn. Have you heard you need to slow down in order to speed up? This is the case for taking captive your thoughts. One to be aware of what you are thinking is first. Second, identify where it came from. Third, does it line up to the word of God and what He has me doing? When you elevate your awareness of the thoughts you are thinking then you begin to only take in what is helping you develop and discarding the clutter sent in to distract. Scripture memory helps in this area.

"Your word I have hidden in my heart, that I might not sin against You." Psalm 119:11

Phase 4 - Dive Deep

This is part one of the foundation zone. Just like building a house or building the most expensive and most important piece is the foundation. There is nothing necessarily attractive about these next two areas. It requires focused effort and perseverance to come out on the other side.

Side note: It is worth the effort. Keep moving forward. I have a saying to keep your shoulders back and your head up. Keep smiling, it will work out.

"But the just shall live by his faith." Habakkuk 2:4b NKJV

This area is more times than not a lonelier and more quiet place. It is the deep soil and the most fertile soil by the way.

We are not dealing with top layer symptoms here. This is where we uproot old habits, patterns, belief systems. We tear down everything that we have exalted which in turn has stifled our process, such as fear, insecurities, antiquated ways and so on.

"But we have renounced the hidden things of shame." 2 Corinthians 4:2 NKJV

This means we need to get rid of the things that would hinder or delay our growth. The scripture says that this is the fertile soil or the good soil. Let's look at what it takes to have good soil. One you need to have all the rocks out of it. Two, you will need to make sure that there are not any weeds that would choke out the seed. This part of the soil is an area that is rich in nutrients and void of harmful objects that would affect the growth. It has to be watered and nurtured.

Activity in this phase is to be conscientious of what is in the soil and remove any hindrances, obstacles and distractions. This phase we will have to uproot old belief systems, patterns or habits that we have held onto. Plus, we need to stop all negative talk, criticism, and skepticism that blocks us from moving forward.

Phase 5 – Deep Dive Part 2

You are on the second half of the stretch. This is where we build and plant. You are focusing on building out new disciplines, new habits and systems to keep you going. Planting seeds for your future, current growth and in outside projects that align to who God has called you to be.

You are in the fertile soil. It is the good soil and this is the time to make a bigger footprint. It is time to expand by getting more knowledge and add to your understanding. This is the time to build and to plant. Using the word of God make declarations of what the Lord says about you and your future. Begin to build yourself up in faith and secure your trust in God. The work that you are putting in for you, your mind, heart and physically takes determination and courage that will bring you through the foundation phase.

"This Book of the Law shall not depart from your mouth, but you

shall meditate in it day and night, that you may observe to do according to all that is written in it. For then you will make your way prosperous, and then you will have good success. Have I not commanded you? Be strong and of good courage; do not be afraid, nor be dismayed, for the LORD your God is with you wherever you go." Joshua 1:8-9 NKJV

Activity in this phase is to meditate on the Word of God. This meditation goes further than mere memorization but it entails processing the scriptures in your heart and mind. The other activity in this phase is declaring what the Lord says about you and your calling. Make sure what comes out of your mouth and into your thoughts is in line with the scriptures.

Phase 6 – Revelation

In the parable of the sower we see some seeds produce 30-fold, 60-fold and 100-fold returns. This phase you will begin to notice things happening. You will be surprised and full of joy as things that you are doing start to take shape. Expect more and more ah-ha moments. You find your strength and endurance building while noticing the situations that set you back in the past now seem to come and go quicker. Your recovery time is faster and you can accomplish more.

"But may the God of all grace, who called us to His eternal glory by Christ Jesus, after you have suffered a while, perfect, establish, strengthen, and settle you." 1 Peter 5:10 NKJV

Activity in this phase is to stay yielded to the process and praise Him for the victory and strength He has given to you. Keep in mind this phase is still on the noise level and keeping yourself fixed on the goal will be valuable for you in this stage.

Phase 7 – Manifestation

You and others begin to notice something is different about you and can see visible changes. You aren't doing what you used to do and the results of your progress become more real and exciting to you. The temptation here is to believe that you are finished and you finally made it; however, this is the starting point and the new you.

Activity in exercising your faith and continuing to do the things that brought you to this point is key to moving forward.

"I press toward the goal for the prize of the upward call of God in Christ Jesus." Philippians 3:14 NKJV

The responsibilities now are beginning to change from the old responsibilities when you first started the process. Here is the place you know the how, what, where and why of the process and the key is to make it a lifestyle. To illustrate this phase is when you have chosen a healthier lifestyle to eat correctly. After establishing a healthy routine and you see the results the goal is to stay the course. This is where you shift from a temporary activity and commit to making this a lifestyle.

Phase 8 – Transformation

You are different in this phase. You can look and see a complete transformation. What was once just a seed has now become a full grown fruit bearing tree. You can't even imagine who you were before. Things are different and you approach and see things differently. The habits and patterns established have become a way of life. This is the Wow Zone. You're super excited that you didn't quit and the whole thing becomes a reality.

"Blessed is the man Who walks not in the counsel of the ungodly, Nor stands in the path of sinners, Nor sits in the seat of the scornful; But his delight is in the law of the Lord, And in His law he meditates day and night. He shall be like a tree Planted by the rivers of water, That brings forth its fruit in its season, Whose leaf also shall not wither; And whatever he does shall prosper." Psalms 1:1-3 NKJV

Activity in this phase, since you created a lifestyle,,,,, is not to become conceited or all knowing. It is our responsibility to continue to call upon the Lord and allow Him to lead us in this area. Yes we are in a completely different place than we were and He is going to continue to move us into areas that require us to grow and help others.

"But we all, with unveiled face, beholding as in a mirror the glory of the Lord, are being transformed into the same image from glory to glory, just as by the Spirit of the Lord." 2 Corinthians 3:18 NKJV

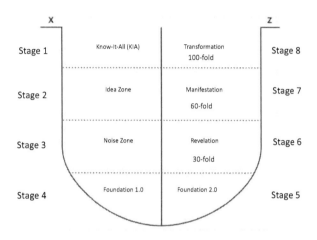

12 YOUR CALLING

"For we are His workmanship, created in Christ Jesus for good works, which God prepared beforehand that we should walk in them." Ephesians 2:10 NKJV

Imagine what it would be like to find an envelope with a letter addressed to you. No return address makes you curious about the sender. You are in a hurry to get to a place where you can open up the envelope and read the letter. The message addressed specifically to you stops you in your tracks. The opening line is "I have known you and ordained you before you were even formed and from this day forward I will reveal who I am as you seek to understand everything that I have planned out for you."

Your heart is racing fast as you are trying to figure out who knew you and what does this all mean. In the next paragraphs you see a commission and mandate to be fulfilled. You notice instructions and a blueprint created just for you to fulfill. This is the letter for you and the life you are called to live. In this letter contains the mystery of your calling and the mission field to which you are called.

The letter goes on to say "Everything that you will need has already been provided; however the caveat is that you will need to seek the sender of the letter for ongoing revelation.

Also, you will be the answer to the prayers of those I am calling you to reach. They will be waiting on your gift to help them resolve the issues that have kept them back."

As you begin this journey you notice that you access supernatural power, wisdom and favor when you remain in harmony with the instructions of the letter. There is an unprecedented peace that surrounds you and guards your heart and mind throughout this journey. There are obstacles and things you need to overcome but the joy of the journey is like fire shut up in your bones.

You find out in this letter are several components that will unlock the mystery of this calling. One, you have to seek the sender. There is a plan, a future and a hope laid out for you from the foundation of the world. Now it is up to you on this journey to find it. Two, in this journey it will be imperative to be in the best overall health as possible. Your eight areas are clearly mapped out and your responsibility in each area will release a heightened level of fortitude. Third, in this letter it clearly says that you will be the answer to the prayers of a particular group of people that you are sent to. It is up to you to develop professionally in order to build the strength, capacity and wherewithal to fulfill the mission and create strategies.

God created you for a specific purpose and has given you the tools and resources to accomplish the task. It's time to discover your calling and how this all fits together. You are called, meaning that God in His infinite wisdom has placed you on earth at the exact time and place to advance His Kingdom. The gifts, talents and skill sets you have acquired up to this point, mixed with your experiences and life events, have brought you here. Your calling possesses the anointing, which is His power associated to your call. As you align with His will and plan you will begin to unlock the blessings and power inside of you.

His anointing breaks the yoke and removes the burden. The yoke represented the hard teaching and ways, and the burden was the emotional toil and drain. The anointing unlocks the power to create a better, more efficient way with the freedom, peace and liberty. As we dive into this part of the journey, I pray your eyes be opened to all that the Lord has in store for you.

"The eyes of your understanding being enlightened; that you may know what is the hope of His calling, what are the riches of the glory of His inheritance in the saints, and what is the exceeding greatness of His power toward us who believe" Ephesians 1:18-19 NKJV

Let's get started. In the book of Jeremiah, the first chapter, God speaks to Jeremiah and tells him that he is ordained a prophet to the nations. As you read your personal letter, you are going to discover that the Lord has a plan for you, and you need to seek it out.

"For I know the plans I have for you," declares the Lord, "plans to prosper you and not to harm you, plans to give you hope and a future." Jeremiah 29:11 NIV

Using the diagram at the end of this chapter we are going to go over several areas to help you identify and map out your calling.

Question 1: If you had enough time and money that you didn't have to work anymore, what would you find yourself doing? The column on the left is the Responsibility column where you should list items such as mortgage, kids, marriage, cars, and everything that you're responsible for. The column on the right is the Luxury Column. This column should show all the luxury items such as traveling, boats, vacations, hobbies, and all of the things you enjoy doing. Write down the luxuries under the luxury column and then write down the responsibilities in the other column.

When you compartmentalize, it becomes easier to prioritize and organize. You begin to realize what is luxury versus responsibility. There is nothing wrong with either column. The concept is to view this from a different lens, which allows you to make the necessary adjustments to experience different results. Compartmentalizing is not the same as isolating separate areas, but understanding how to highlight a particular area and then plug it back into the whole. This exercise will help you identify each area and the functionality within the whole picture.

As you go through these exercises you will begin to see things as a whole and become more conscientious of how to compartmentalize so you can manage more efficiently. Discernment is a gift of the Holy Spirit and helps us decipher. Once we have identified the items in both columns we can move to the center, which is our purpose. Moving closer to the center of the will of God for our lives keeps us aligned correctly to the assignment for us to fulfill. I often say, be in alignment to your assignment.

Question 2: If you had enough time and money, you no longer had to work, and you had to contribute back to humanity, what would you find yourself doing? Write down your answer(s) under the Purpose column which is in the center. The envelope is your purpose. It is hidden for you to seek it out and then discover how to fulfill it. This reveals what you are passionate about whether it is volunteering, giving back or educating. This area resonates in your heart on what you are called to solve or help or build.

The good news here is the purpose of God evolves as you continue to walk out your journey, so just pick a place that resonates with you to get started. For example, you may have a heart to work with youth or the homeless. As you go you will grow, and the Lord will guide and direct your steps.

"Trust in the Lord with all your heart, And lean not on your own understanding; In all your ways acknowledge Him, And He shall direct your paths." Proverbs 3:5-6 NKJV

Our understanding is only in part and as we press into the Lord and His word He will broaden our understanding. Let's break the word understanding down.

The word under and the word standing. What are we standing on? If your knowledge was the foundation of where your feet were planted how large would that be? As we increase the foundation we actually broaden the place where we stand or translated into that we have a larger place to stand on.

In this process there are three essential elements when identifying what you are called to do that will help you navigate. These areas I will illustrate with the diagram so you can see how they work collectively together and will help define the roles and expectations. Dependence is the first element. When it comes to purpose, we need to remain completely dependent on God. He is the author and finisher of our faith and His thoughts and ways are higher than our thoughts and ways.

Independence is the second element. There is a part that is your responsibility in this equation. God gives us the assignment and the ability to accomplish the task at hand and it is our responsibility to steward the process internally and externally.

"His divine power has given to us all things that pertain to life and godliness, through the knowledge of Him who called us by glory and virtue" 2 Peter 1:3 NKJV

We have been given everything we need for life and godliness. The Lord will instruct us to go, to stay, pray, to speak and we need to be ready. We need to be able to do our part and trust the Lord.

"Preach the word of God. Be prepared, whether the time is favorable or not. Patiently correct, rebuke, and encourage your people with good teaching." 2 Timothy 4:2 NLT

Interdependence is the third area. This area requires steady growth. You will notice as you progress in walking out your calling that people will come in for a reason, season or lifetime. Plus, the tools, resources or money that were necessary to launch may or may not be the same amount required to sustain or scale. This is where we can stretch to have a greater reach, impact and influence.

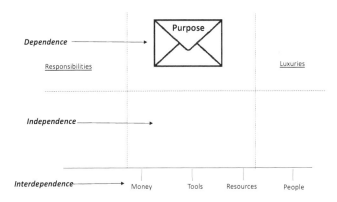

"Enlarge the place of your tent, And let them stretch out the curtains of your dwellings; Do not spare; lengthen your cords and strengthen your stakes. for you shall expand to the right and to the left, And your descendants will inherit the nations, and make the desolate cities

inhabited." Isaiah 54:2-3 NKJV

Along with personal development or working on ourselves we need to look at the items on the bottom line of the diagram which we can categorize as professional development. At the time I was working on this myself, drawing this out allowed me to look at it from a different angle, giving me a new perspective of how it all works. I knew that if God gave me a vision there has to be provision (money) used to fund the vision. Compensation, overhead, expenses and giving out of surplus, I needed a budget and plan. My job was to increase my knowledge regarding Biblical wealth and pray for the right strategies to implement.

Tools and resources such as digital media, graphics, technologies plus a library to get help or answers are other necessary components to acquire. These tools can help grow your knowledge base and create the infrastructure necessary to automate and delegate to increase efficiency. The need to acquire tools and resources will grow as you grow. The important part is to start with what you have in your hand and let the Lord bless the work.

Regardless of your assignment, you will need people. Those who mentor, those who assist, those who have done something similar. We were created by God to work together with others. God will align us with the right community as we continue to work out our faith and have the passion to fulfill our purpose.

"Where there is no counsel, the people fall; But in the multitude of

counselors there is safety." Proverbs 11:14 NKJV

As you grow you begin to identify the places where you need more attention, focus and energy. Plus, you will need to create priorities based through the filter of your calling. Things that are top priority now may not be at the top of the list when you change how you look at this down the road. The intentionality for the task at hand increases more and more as you gain the confidence and know how.

Your Unique Stamp on Life

Once you have started working on the diagram and mapping out the different sections it is time to delve into more areas. You as an individual were created in His image according to His likeness. What does that mean? As a person you carry a special gift mix and talents orchestrated by God to be an asset to your community and the Body of Christ. There is one body with many parts. Your unique stamp on life is composed of your style, value system, passion, and community. This is your unique personal brand.

Your Style

Another activity worth looking into is defining your style and how you operate. I work with my clients through workshops and individually to help them identify how they react, respond and receive. Regardless of the setting, be it a church, corporation or non-profit, I have seen such great revelation come out of teaching about style. How do you communicate and what are your natural or adaptive tendencies? My clients gain a deeper understanding but also a higher level of comfort in knowing who they are.

A personality profile such as Myers Briggs or the DISC Assessment studies and analyzes your reactions and how you respond to everyday life in detail. It basically answers the question of *What makes me tick?* Once you are cognizant of how you react, respond, and receive you will have a better understanding of what is fulfilling. Furthermore, you can begin to hone into making any improvements and utilizing your strengths.

Discovering and understanding your own personality traits gives you the advantage of making decisions that best fit you and your goals. A personality profile takes a comprehensive look on who you think you are, who you actually are, and how others might see you. I have used several types of personality profiles to help identify my communication and personality style. A deeper understanding in your personal communication style and how you operate gives way to having a better understanding of how others react and respond.

"I have become all things to all men, that I might by all means save some." 1 Corinthians 9:22 NKJV

Core Values

Defining your core values is a liberating exercise. Having the ability to articulate your values establishes a strong filtering system. Sometimes it is helpful to figure out the things that really upset you. If you would take the antithesis of the root cause of whatever upset you, then you are well on your way to identifying your core values. This step is often overlooked as individuals and rarely written down. However, many companies have their core values visibly displayed. This serves as a great value to keep them top-of-mind. Also, have their value system posted where everyone can see and memorize them. As an individual, your core values determine your habits and your habits determine your character.

Your core values will stem from the way you see things. Your world view, healthy or unhealthy, directly affects your decisions. This is important when looking at our value system, because it's also a filter moving forward. Good news. Wherever you are, you can always get a healthy world view when we turn to God and ask Him to give us eyes to see.

"I have not stopped thanking God for you. I pray for you constantly, asking God, the glorious Father of our Lord Jesus Christ, to give you spiritual wisdom and insight so that you might grow in your knowledge of God." Ephesians 1:16-17 NLT

Developing your personal brand is exciting and challenging at the same time. The exciting part is being able to walk into the person who God has already called you to be. The challenging aspect is identifying and peeling away the layers that have been added to our lives either through our upbringing, belief systems, environment or connections. The Bible is clear when it says that broad is the road that leads to destruction and narrow is the way that leads to life. It is ultimately our faith that determines our core values.

"For where your treasure is, there your heart will be also." Matthew 6:21

Your Passion

What things are you passionate about? It is one thing to talk about a particular subject manner and it is completely different when you light up with enthusiasm whenever you are asked to comment. Your passion brings about such a force of energy that resonates at a higher frequency than most other things. Such as, if you have a heart for youth and you find yourself spending a large portion of your time working in programs with them. You could be passionate about creating programs to feed the hungry in your area. There are so many avenues and when you find identify your giftings then there is the anointing from God to allow you to perform at high levels in your calling.

Your Community

Be intentional on building your community. This group of people share similar objectives and passions in life as you. To be successful and help others do the same. Your community will have those who become mentors, those who are mentees and encouragers. This group provides encouragement to continue moving forward. You will also find wisdom in the counsel of many in this group. Plus, there is a protection that this community provides as you do life with them. I have defined and redefined my community numerous times. I have found the more focused I am in who I surround myself with the better I become in all areas. Your calling is directly associated with a community of people. Together as a unified group you have the ability to influence culture and increase your impact on lives you come into contact with.

Your Message

Your message is your story that combines your passion with your core values and is written to bring about the change that God has put into your heart to bring about. The life experiences and lessons that you have learned, and the passion that is in your heart, need to be released. In the beginning God spoke and it happened. Since you and I are created in His image and according to His likeness we also carry the creative power when we release or speak our message.

As we look back into our lives there were moments that we were able to dream and too often as adults we lose that ability to dream due to life circumstances. This is the time to tap back into the dreams you had when you were younger. This reveals hidden nuggets to propel you to create this story. In your journey you have multiple experiences and life lessons tucked away in the memory banks of your mind. Now, as you take an introspective look and begin to write down what you are passionate about your eyes will be tuned to see your calling. This story comes from your heart and resonates with the people who it is supposed to touch. It is what I call a heart-cord. When you are able to compose your heart-cord story, the power released is life-giving to the hearers.

Too many times we can go through our daily routines and forget that each of us is individually unique. We have so much to offer and the value that we bring to our family, friends, co-workers, customers and community is often greater than we realize. What makes us different and unique? When we dig beyond the surface, past the bills, daily responsibilities and find that small longing to do something meaningful. It is at that point where passion comes alive and purpose is born. How do we make this dream into a reality? The inner longing needs a voice and that is You! It needs your past and present experiences. It is clothed and takes shape with your struggles, trials and victories. Life doesn't deal us the perfect hand and we have heard that when you are given lemons turn it into lemonade. So, tell your story and allow the things that you have been through, good-bad-indifferent, be the catalyst to expressing your story. Everyone enjoys hearing stories and it is our story that truly represents who we are and what we are about.

After conducting a workshop on Your Unique Brand and Signature Message, I had one of the attendees reach out to me to share her experience. She admitted to being a little hesitant at first to combine her passion with her business. Not knowing what the reaction would be, she yielded to the process and wrote out her signature message. An opportunity arose to speak to an organization with which she was affiliated, and she told me that she used her signature message. After the meeting she was approached by a woman in the audience who told her how powerful the message was and how much it resonated with her. The woman then proceeded to ask my client if she would mind if the woman's company could put her as a top resource partner because she likes to work with others who share similar passions. My client was more than excited—one to share her story, and two to have an opportunity to grow her business.

"Be faithful to pray as intercessors who are fully alert and giving thanks to God. And please pray for me, that God will open a door of opportunity for us to preach the revelation of the mystery of Christ, for whose sake I am imprisoned. Pray that I would unfold and reveal fully this mystery, for that is my delightful assignment." Colossians 4:2-4 TPT

You have a story. What are you passionate about? Is there something that you would like to see changed, corrected or rebuilt? These are the areas that I look for when helping someone craft their signature message. What makes you tick and gets you excited? Putting a voice with an actionable plan together in a form of a message is one of the greatest gifts you can give. Your story shared in the hearts of others to help them get free from things that they struggle with. Teach them a new skill to help them succeed. Help them discover methods that would bring restoration and hope to them and others. This story that you have on the inside of you once spoken goes out further than you can compute. Your story written is stored and passed down to generations to come. This is your legacy.

This is expanding your impact on society. What has the Lord put into your heart to accomplish?

"Death and life are in the power of the tongue, And those who love it will eat its fruit." Proverbs 18:21 NKJV

Hold fast to His promise. He is faithful and the promise will come. As you share your story door will open and you will begin to identify more places where the Lord is directing you.

It's time to take the next step. Get plugged into a ministry, church or place that has the audience you desire to help. Find somewhere to get involved with helping and exercising your gifts. No more sitting on the sidelines. It is time to rise up with the message that the Lord has graciously put into your heart. *"For you were raised for such a time as this." Esther 4:14 NKJV*

This is not the end but only the beginning. God has amazing things in store for us. New territory, visions and promises to reach out and grab. As you move forward, it is my desire to see you grow in your walk with the Lord, know your calling and fulfill it to the advancing of His Kingdom. Use this book as a guide and reference to help propel you on your journey with God. We serve a loving and faithful God, and what He starts in us He is faithful to complete. May God bless you on your journey, and I look forward to hearing your story!

SUMMARY CHECKLIST

Battery Pack – Life Score

1. _____ Score yourself according to your perception in each area.

2. _____ Get your overall Life-Score average.

3. _____ Identify three key areas which need improvement.

4. _____ Monitor your score quarterly or semi-annually.

Take Action

5. _____ Identify 1-3 activities in each area that could use improving.

6. _____ Create your pathway by mapping out the before, during and after the process of the activity prior to implementing. This will assist you in keeping you focused.

7. _____ Be consistent in the activities you start,

measuring progress and momentum.

8. _____ Once you improve your score then begin to roll in other areas in your day-to-day activities.

Power of the Process

9. _____ Write down three areas where you would like to see major results.

10. _____ Review the eight phases and identify where you are in each of the areas you are working on.

11. _____ Write out the area and what you need to focus on according to the Eight Phases of Transformation.

Purpose Diagram

12. _____ Establish a clear view of your Purpose as it relates to your Luxuries and Responsibilities.

13. _____ List the responsibilities and luxuries in their separate columns.

14. _____ Write out your Purpose, or what you are passionate about to contribute back to society.

15. _____ Identify the areas of Dependence, Independence and Interdependence.

16. _____ Describe what your activity needs to be with each area.

17. _____ Identify the four elements on the horizontal plane of the Purpose Diagram.

18. _____ Write your current needs regarding tools, resources, finances and connections.

Unique Brand Identifier

19. _____ Identify four areas that make up your Unique Brand Identifier.

20. _____ Using a personality assessment, describe your style and how you react.

21. _____ Write out your core values and how you would describe each one individually.

22. _____ Describe what you are passionate about in two to three sentences.

23. _____ Explain who is in your community and the similarities to your calling.

Your Message

24. _____ Write what you would like for your message to accomplish.

25. _____ Determine and write a description of your ideal audience for your message.

26. _____ Identify and write down where you can plug in and get involved.

27. _____ Write out a plan on how to get your message across.

God has amazing things in store for you. God bless you on your journey!

"May the Lord bless you and protect you. May the Lord smile on you and be gracious to you. May the Lord show you his favor and give you his peace."
Numbers 6:24-26 NLT

ADDITIONAL WORKSHEETS

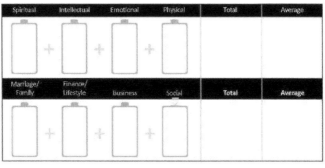

Spiritual	Intellectual	Emotional	Physical	Total	Average

Marriage/ Family	Finance/ Lifestyle	Business	Social	Total	Average

Overall Operation Score:

_____   _____
Total   Average

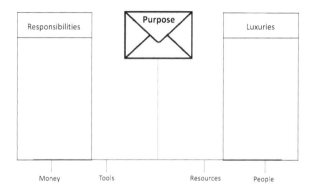

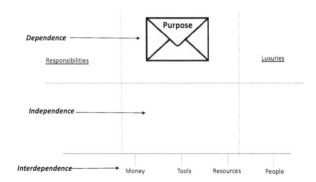

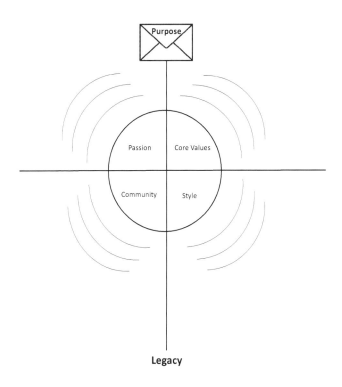

Legacy